Selenium WebDriver Practical Guide

Interactively automate web applications using Selenium WebDriver

Satya Avasarala

BIRMINGHAM - MUMBAI

Selenium WebDriver Practical Guide

Copyright © 2014 Packt Publishing

First published: January 2014

Production Reference: 1170114

Published by Packt Publishing Ltd.
Livery Place
35 Livery Street
Birmingham B3 2PB, UK.

ISBN 978-1-78216-885-0

www.packtpub.com

Cover Image by Prashant Timappa Shetty (sparkling.spectrum.123@gmail.com)

Credits

Author
Satya Avasarala

Reviewers
Anuj Chaudhary
David Askirk Fotel
Daniel Lam
Ripon Al Wasim

Acquisition Editors
Anthony Albuquerque
Richard Harvey

Lead Technical Editor
Priya Singh

Technical Editors
Dennis John
Venu Manthena
Gaurav Thingalaya

Copy Editors
Tanvi Gaitonde
Kirti Pai
Adithi Shetty

Project Coordinator
Amey Sawant

Proofreader
Clyde Jenkins

Indexers
Hemangini Bari
Monica Ajmera Mehta
Rekha Nair
Priya Subramani

Graphics
Yuvraj Mannari
Abhinash Sahu

Production Coordinator
Aparna Bhagat

Cover Work
Aparna Bhagat

About the Author

Satya Avasarala has rich experience in Java development and automation testing. He is an engineer in computer science. He has used WebDriver for many years now and has created several good automation frameworks. He has worked at various large software enterprises such as Oracle Corp, Yahoo! Inc., VMware Inc., and the REA Group.

In addition, he is also interested in Service Oriented Architectural design and Business Intelligence. He is an Oracle-certified Service Oriented Architecture Infrastructure Implementation Expert and a Business Intelligence Foundation Suite Implementation Specialist.

I would like to thank all my acquisition editors, technical editors, and project coordinators for constantly supporting me in completing this book. I should also thank my colleagues, Pratik Patil and Kerri Rusnak, for their constant encouragement and support in writing this book. Last but not least, I would like to thank my wife, Swathi Vennelaganti, for sacrificing many weekends while I was busy writing this book. Without all these people, this book wouldn't have been a reality.

About the Reviewers

Anuj Chaudhary is a software engineer who enjoys working on software testing and automation. He has a vast experience with various testing methodologies such as manual testing, automated testing, performance testing, and security testing. He has worked as an individual contributor and technical lead on various software projects dealing with all of the stages in the application development life cycle.

He has been awarded the title of Microsoft MVP twice in a row. He writes a blog that you can visit at www.anujchaudhary.com.

> I would like to thank and congratulate the Packt Publishing team for publishing this awesome book.

David Askirk Fotel has worked with computers since his parents brought home an old, used IBM PS/2. He started his development career writing simple programs in QBasic and later in Pascal. From there, he moved on to writing programs in C. Later on, he moved on to Java and other languages. His greatest experience so far was with Lisp, which had a great impact on his programming style and approach to code.

David has worked on test-driven development and as a test manager, implementing Selenium tests on an e-learning system.

This book is the first on which David has worked, but will not be the last!

Daniel Lam is an Agile Test Developer with experience in open and closed source test tools. He specializes in Java, Selenium WebDriver, Continuous Integration, and BDD test frameworks.

Ripon Al Wasim is a software engineer living in Dhaka, Bangladesh. He has 12 years' experience in the software industry, three years in software development, and nine years in software testing (both manual and automated). He has also been involved in conducting software testing courses in various companies. He has worked for clients in various countries such as Japan, USA, Finland, Norway, and Bangladesh.

Ripon started participating in posting professional questions and answers on Stack Overflow in the year 2011 at `http://stackoverflow.com/users/617450/ripon-al-wasim`.

Ripon is a Sun Certified Java Programmer (SCJP). He is Japanese Language Proficiency Test (JLPT) Level 3 certified, and is a little familiar with Japanese culture, as he stayed in Japan for one year as an IT professional. This book is Ripon's first official effort.

I would like to thank my mother and wife for fostering a helping and inspiring environment at home so I could study and review. I am also deeply thankful and grateful to Cefalo Amravi Ltd. (`http://cefalo.com/en`), my current company, for providing me a good opportunity to work with automated testing using Selenium WebDriver. I would like to thank Yves Hwang, Product Manager at Varnish Software (`https://www.varnish-software.com/`) and Partha Guha Roy, CTO of Cefalo Amravi Ltd. for providing technical assistance during my project work.

www.PacktPub.com

Support files, eBooks, discount offers and more

You might want to visit www.PacktPub.com for support files and downloads related to your book.

Did you know that Packt offers eBook versions of every book published, with PDF and ePub files available? You can upgrade to the eBook version at www.PacktPub.com and as a print book customer, you are entitled to a discount on the eBook copy. Get in touch with us at service@packtpub.com for more details.

At www.PacktPub.com, you can also read a collection of free technical articles, sign up for a range of free newsletters and receive exclusive discounts and offers on Packt books and eBooks.

http://PacktLib.PacktPub.com

Do you need instant solutions to your IT questions? PacktLib is Packt's online digital book library. Here, you can access, read and search across Packt's entire library of books.

Why Subscribe?

- Fully searchable across every book published by Packt
- Copy and paste, print and bookmark content
- On demand and accessible via web browser

Free Access for Packt account holders

If you have an account with Packt at www.PacktPub.com, you can use this to access PacktLib today and view nine entirely free books. Simply use your login credentials for immediate access.

Table of Contents

Preface

This book is about Selenium WebDriver, also known as Selenium 2, which is a UI automation tool used by software developers and QA engineers to test their web application on different web browsers. The reader is expected to have a basic idea of programming, preferably using Java, because we take the reader through several features of WebDriver using code examples. This book can be used as a reference for your day-to-day usage of WebDriver.

What this book covers

Chapter 1, Introducing WebDriver and WebElements, will start off by briefly discussing the history of Selenium and the differences between Selenium 1 and Selenium 2. Then, we quickly jump into WebDriver by describing how it perceives a web page. We will also look at what a WebDriver's WebElement is. Then, we talk about locating WebElements on a web page and performing some basic actions on them.

Chapter 2, Exploring Advanced Interactions of WebDriver, will dive deeply into more advanced actions that WebDriver can perform on the WebElements of a web page, such as the dragging-and-dropping of elements from one frame of a page to another and right/context-clicking on WebElements. We're sure you will find this chapter interesting to read.

Chapter 3, Exploring the Features of WebDriver, will talk about some advanced features of WebDriver, such as taking screenshots of web pages, executing JavaScript, and handling cookies and proxies.

Chapter 4, Different Available WebDrivers, will talk about various implementations of WebDriver, such as FirefoxDriver, IEDriver, and ChromeDriver. When we discuss WebDriver in *Chapter 1, Introducing WebDriver and WebElements*, we will see that WebDriver has specific implementations for most of the popular browsers available on the market.

Chapter 5, Understanding WebDriver Events, will deal with the event-handling aspect of WebDriver. To state a few, events can be a value change on a WebElement, a browser back-navigation invocation, script execution completion, and so on.

Chapter 6, Dealing with I/O, will introduce you to the file-handling features of WebDriver. Concepts such as copying files, uploading files, and deleting files will be discussed in this chapter.

Chapter 7, Exploring RemoteWebDriver and WebDriverBackedSelenium, will deal with two very important topics of WebDriver: RemoteWebDriver and WebDriverBackedSelenium. If you want to execute a WebDriver installed on a different machine from your machine, you can use the RemoteWebDriver class to handle all your commands for that remote machine. One of its popular use cases is browser compatibility testing. The other class we talk about in this chapter is WebDriverBackedSelenium. This is useful for people who want to use WebDriver, but still have many of their existing tests using Selenium 1. Finally, we will migrate some code using Selenium1 APIs to use WebDriver APIs.

Chapter 8, Understanding Selenium Grid, will talk about one important and interesting feature of Selenium named Selenium Grid. Using this, you can submit your developed automation scenarios to a server and specify there the target platform, that is, the OS, browser type, and version, upon which you want these scenarios to be executed. If a node with such a configuration is registered and available, the server will dispatch your job to that node, and it will take care of executing your automation scenarios in its environment and publish the results back to the server.

Chapter 9, Understanding PageObject Pattern, will talk about a well-known design pattern named the PageObject pattern. This is a proven pattern that will give you a better handle on your automation framework and scenarios.

Chapter 10, Testing iOS and Android Apps, we will take you through how WebDriver can be used to automate your test scripts for iOS and Android applications. We will also discuss a recently developed software tool called Appium.

By the end of this book, we are sure you will be one of the world's advanced WebDriver users.

What you need for this book

The following sections describe the installation of components required to work with the code in this book.

Installing Java

In this book, all the code examples that we show covering various features of WebDriver will be in Java. To follow these examples and write your own code, you need Java Development Kit installed on your computer. The latest version of JDK can be downloaded from the following link:

```
http://docs.oracle.com/javase/7/docs/webnotes/install/windows/jdk-
installation-windows.html
```

A step-by-step installation guide is available at the following link:

```
http://docs.oracle.com/javase/7/docs/webnotes/install/windows/jdk-
installation-windows.html
```

Installing Eclipse

This book is a practical guide that expects the user to write and execute WebDriver examples. For this, it would be handy to install a Java IDE. You can install your favorite IDE. Here, I am installing Eclipse. It can be downloaded from the following link:

```
http://www.eclipse.org/downloads/packages/eclipse-ide-java-
developers/junosr2
```

Installing Firefox

Most of the work in this book will be done using Firefox. However, we do talk about other browsers and their respective drivers in *Chapter 4, Different Available WebDrivers*. We will work with Firefox 17.0.1, which has been tested and tried against WebDriver 2.33.0. It can be downloaded from the following link:

```
https://ftp.mozilla.org/pub/mozilla.org/firefox/releases/17.0.1/
```

Installing Firebug

Firebug is one of the add-ons of Firefox. It is widely used to inspect HTML elements on a web page. You can get Firebug from the following link:

```
https://getfirebug.com/
```

After installation, when you open the Firefox browser, you should see the firebug icon on the top-right corner of the browser, as shown highlighted in red in the following screenshot:

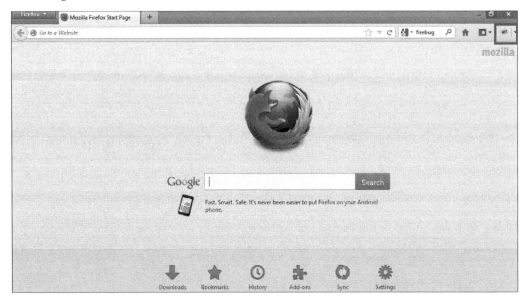

Now, click on the Firebug icon to load the Firebug UI, as shown in the following screenshot:

Installing FirePath

After you have installed the Firebug add-on to Firefox, it's time to extend Firebug to have something named FirePath. FirePath is used to get XPath and CSS values of an HTML element on a web page. You can download FirePath from the following location:

```
https://addons.mozilla.org/en-US/firefox/addon/FirePath/
```

After installation, you should see a new tab in the Firebug UI for FirePath, as shown in the following screenshot:

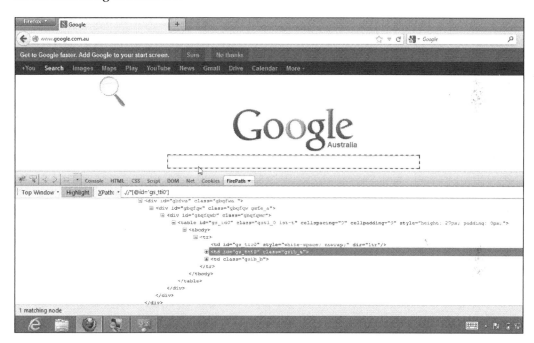

Downloading WebDriver client library (language bindings)

As discussed earlier, test scripts need a client library with which to interact, or command WebDriver to execute specific user events against a web application being tested on a browser. For this, you need to download the WebDriver client library. In this book, we use Java language bindings to create and execute our automation scripts.

At the time of writing this book, all the code examples are written based on Selenium Java Version 2.33.0. It is recommended that you download that version from the following location:

```
https://code.google.com/p/selenium/downloads/detail?name=selenium-
java-2.33.0.zip&can=2&q=
```

Downloading the Firefox Driver

The good news is that you have already downloaded the Firefox Driver. Yes, the Firefox Driver comes along with client libraries. But, for other drivers, such as the IE Driver, Safari Driver, Chrome Driver, and so on, you have to download them explicitly from the following link:

```
http://docs.seleniumhq.org/download/
```

We will download them when we need to in *Chapter 4, Different Available WebDrivers*.

Who this book is for

If you are a quality assurance/testing professional, software developer, or web application developer looking to create automation test scripts for your web applications, this is the perfect guide for you! As a prerequisite, this book expects you to have a basic understanding of Java programming, although any previous knowledge of WebDriver or Selenium 1 is not needed. By the end of this book, you will have acquired a comprehensive knowledge of WebDriver, which will help you in writing your automation tests.

Conventions

In this book, you will find a number of styles of text that distinguish among different kinds of information. Here are some examples of these styles, and an explanation of their meaning.

Code words in text, database table names, folder names, filenames, file extensions, pathnames, dummy URLs, user input, and Twitter handles are shown as follows: "The `moveByOffset()` method is used to move the mouse from its current position to another point on the web page."

A block of code is set as follows:

```
public class NavigateToAUrl {
    public static void main(String[] args){
        WebDriver driver = new FirefoxDriver();
```

```
        driver.get("http://www.google.com");
    }
}
```

When we wish to draw your attention to a particular part of a code block, the relevant lines or items are set in bold:

```
public class GoogleSearchButtonByName {
  public static void main(String[] args){
    WebDriver driver = new FirefoxDriver();
    driver.get("http://www.google.com");
    WebElement searchBox = driver.findElement(By.name("btnK"));
    searchBox.submit();
  }
}
```

Any command-line input or output is written as follows:

```
java -jar selenium-server-standalone-2.33.0.jar -role node -hub
  http://172.16.87.131:1111/grid/register -registerCycle 10000
```

New terms and **important words** are shown in bold. Words that you see on the screen, in menus or dialog boxes for example, appear in the text like this: "Open Eclipse from the directory you have installed it in earlier. Navigate to **File | New | Java Project**".

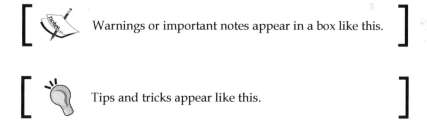

Warnings or important notes appear in a box like this.

Tips and tricks appear like this.

Reader feedback

Feedback from our readers is always welcome. Let us know what you think about this book — what you liked or may have disliked. Reader feedback is important for us to develop titles that you really get the most out of.

To send us general feedback, simply send an e-mail to feedback@packtpub.com, and mention the book title via the subject of your message.

If there is a topic that you have expertise in and you are interested in either writing or contributing to a book, see our author guide on www.packtpub.com/authors.

Customer support

Now that you are the proud owner of a Packt book, we have a number of things to help you to get the most from your purchase.

Downloading the example code

You can download the example code files for all Packt books you have purchased from your account at http://www.packtpub.com. If you purchased this book elsewhere, you can visit http://www.packtpub.com/support and register to have the files e-mailed directly to you.

Errata

Although we have taken every care to ensure the accuracy of our content, mistakes do happen. If you find a mistake in one of our books—maybe a mistake in the text or the code—we would be grateful if you would report this to us. By doing so, you can save other readers from frustration and help us improve subsequent versions of this book. If you find any errata, please report them by visiting http://www.packtpub.com/submit-errata, selecting your book, clicking on the **errata submission form** link, and entering the details of your errata. Once your errata are verified, your submission will be accepted and the errata will be uploaded on our website, or added to any list of existing errata, under the Errata section of that title. Any existing errata can be viewed by selecting your title from http://www.packtpub.com/support.

Piracy

Piracy of copyright material on the Internet is an ongoing problem across all media. At Packt, we take the protection of our copyright and licenses very seriously. If you come across any illegal copies of our works, in any form, on the Internet, please provide us with the location address or website name immediately so that we can pursue a remedy.

Please contact us at copyright@packtpub.com with a link to the suspected pirated material.

We appreciate your help in protecting our authors, and our ability to bring you valuable content.

Questions

You can contact us at questions@packtpub.com if you are having a problem with any aspect of the book, and we will do our best to address it.

1
Introducing WebDriver and WebElements

In this chapter, we will look briefly into the Selenium history and proceed to the basic components of a web page, **WebElements**. We will learn different ways to locate WebElements on a web page and execute various user actions on them. We will cover the following topics in this chapter:

- History of Selenium
- Difference between Selenium 1 and Selenium 2
- Setting up an Eclipse project to execute the example code
- Locating WebElements on a web page
- Actions that can be taken on the WebElements

Understanding the history of Selenium

Though this book is not intended to deal with Selenium 1, it is a good idea to know briefly about it before we start off with WebDriver. In this way, we can understand how and why WebDriver has evolved.

Selenium 1 or Selenium Remote Control or Selenium RC

Selenium RC is a popular UI automation library, allowing developers and testers to automate their interactions with a **Web Application Under Test (WAUT)** by providing them with the necessary libraries, supported in multiple languages, to program.

In terms of design, Selenium RC chose to use generic JavaScript named **Selenium Core** to drive the WAUT on a browser. However, the decision of using generic JavaScript that can drive the WAUT on any browser should comply with a security policy named **Same-Origin Policy**. Every available browser in the market imposes this policy on the websites that are loaded on it.

To know about this policy, we should take a closer look at how a browser executes JavaScript loaded from a website. For every website that is loaded on it, the browser creates a separate sandbox for the website's JavaScript, which restricts the JavaScript to be executed only on it's respective website domain. This way, a JavaScript that belongs to one website doesn't execute on another website that is currently loaded on that browser. This security vulnerability, named **Cross-site scripting**, is the browser's responsibility to restrict. So, coming back to Selenium RC, its generic JavaScript is not allowed, by the browser, to execute on a website (WAUT) that is coming from a different domain.

So, how did Selenium RC handle this? To overcome this security restriction, Selenium RC acts as an HTTP Proxy Server. When the test script asks to launch a browser, Selenium RC server launches the browser and injects its JavaScript (Selenium Core) into the browser. All the subsequent requests for the WAUT go through Selenium RC (acting as an HTTP Proxy Server) to the actual web server hosting WAUT. Thus making the browser think that the web application is being served from the Selenium RC's server domain than the actual web server's domain and allowing Selenium Core to execute and drive the web application.

Typically, it works in the following way:

1. A tester or a developer, through his/her test script, can command Selenium RC server to perform certain actions on the WAUT on a certain browser. The way the user can command Selenium RC to perform something is by using the client libraries provided by Selenium RC. These libraries are provided in different languages, such as Java, Ruby, Python, Perl, PHP, and .NET. These commands, which are passed from the test scripts to Selenium RC, are named **Selenese** commands. In a test script, you will have a set of Selenese commands to test a scenario on the WAUT.

2. Once the Selenium RC server receives the command from the test script, it will launch the test script preferred browser, and while launching, it injects the Selenium Core into the browser.

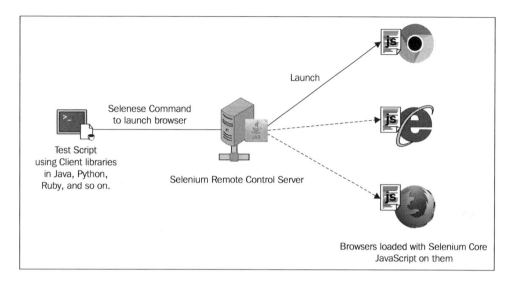

3. Upon loading on the browser, Selenium Core executes all the Selenese commands from the test script, coming through Selenium RC, against the WAUT. The browser doesn't restrict it, because it treats Selenium Core and WAUT as a part of the same domain.

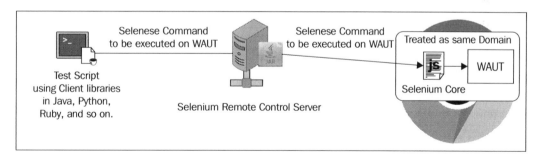

4. Now comes the HTTP Proxy part of the Selenium RC server. All the requests and responses of the browser for WAUT go to the actual web server via Selenium RC server, because the browser thinks Selenium RC is serving WAUT.

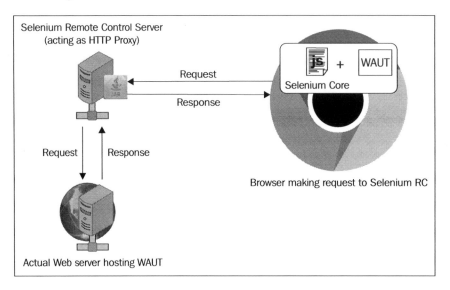

5. After execution, Selenium RC will send out the test result back to the test script for developer's analysis.

Selenium 2 or Selenium WebDriver or WebDriver

To overcome some of the limitations of Selenium 1, which we are going to discuss shortly, WebDriver has come into existence for the following reasons:

- To give a better control on the browser by implementing browser-specific implementations.

- To give a better programming experience to the developer by adhering more closely to the object-oriented programming fundamentals.

It works in the following way:

1. A tester or developer, through his/her test script, can command WebDriver to perform certain actions on the WAUT on a certain browser. The way the user can command WebDriver to perform something is by using the client libraries or language bindings provided by WebDriver. These libraries are provided in different languages, such as Java, Ruby, Python, Perl, PHP, and .NET.

2. By using the language-binding client libraries, developers can invoke the browser-specific implementations of WebDriver, such as Firefox Driver, IE Driver, Opera Driver, and so on, to interact with the WAUT on the respective browser. These browser-specific implementations of WebDriver will work with the browser natively and execute commands from outside the browser to simulate exactly how the application user does.

3. After execution, WebDriver will send out the test result back to the test script for developer's analysis.

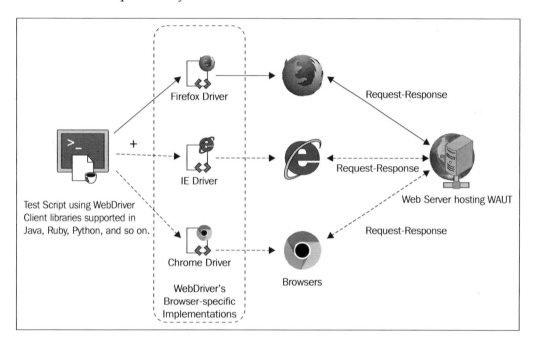

Differences between Selenium 1 and Selenium 2

Now that we know how Selenium 1 and Selenium 2 are designed, let's quickly see the differences between them.

Handling the browser

As we saw earlier, Selenium RC drives the browser from within the browser by sitting in it as JavaScript (Selenium Core). All the events that are to be executed on the WAUT go through Core. This kind of approach will come with some limitations, such as:

- Core being limited within the JavaScript sandbox of the browser, as it needs to comply with the Same-Origin policy.
- Because this JavaScript library is generic and not specific to any particular browser, the developers of test scripts sometimes end up with a situation where their test scripts execute very well on some browsers but not on some other.

To overcome this limitation, WebDriver, on the other hand, handles the browser from outside the browser. It has an implementation for each browser, and the developer who wants to execute his/her tests on a particular browser should use that particular implementation of WebDriver. This gives the test scripts a better handle on the browser because these WebDriver implementations speak to the browsers natively, thus increasing the robustness of the test scripts.

Having better APIs

WebDriver comes with a better set of APIs meeting the expectations of most developers by being closer to the object-oriented programming in terms of its implementation.

Testing mobile apps

Using WebDriver's mobile-specific implementations, such as IPhoneDriver and AndroidDriver, developers can actually generate test scripts that can execute their mobile applications on simulators/emulators and actual devices. Selenium RC doesn't support mobile application testing.

Having developer support and advanced functionalities

WebDriver is being actively developed over a period of time, and you can see many advanced interactions with the web as well as mobile applications, such as File Handling, Touch APIs, and so on. The API set of it is getting bigger and bigger with lots of features, which were never thought about in Selenium RC. Definitely, it is the future!

Setting up a project in Eclipse

Now, let's set up our project in Eclipse and write our first piece of code to use WebDriver and navigate to a web page. Please follow the sequence of the following steps to create an Eclipse WebDriver project:

1. Open Eclipse from the directory you have installed it in earlier. Navigate to **File** | **New** | **Java Project**.

2. A **New Java Project** dialog appears, as shown in the following screenshot. Enter the project name of your choice, leave the rest to default, and click **Next**.

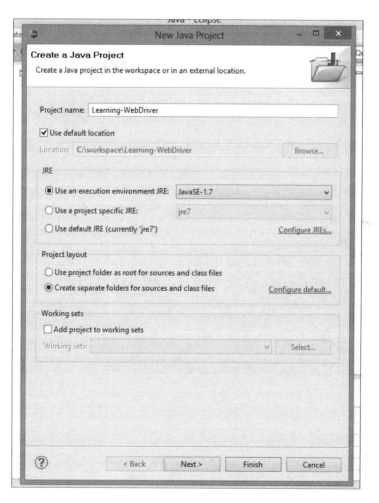

3. In the next screen, go to the **Libraries** tab, click on the **Add External JARs...** button, and select `selenium-java-2.33.0.jar` and `selenium-java-2.33.0-srcs.jar` files from the downloaded location of Selenium WebDriver.

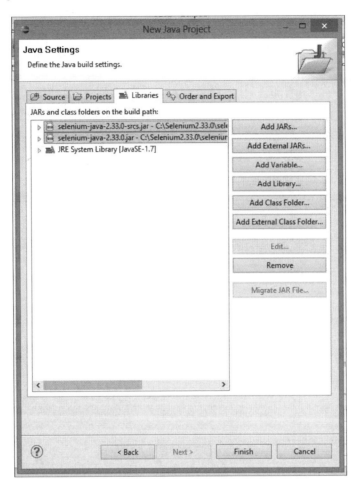

4. Click on the **Add External JARs...** button and add all the jars available under the `libs` folder of the Selenium WebDriver directory(). Now the **Libraries** section should look like this:

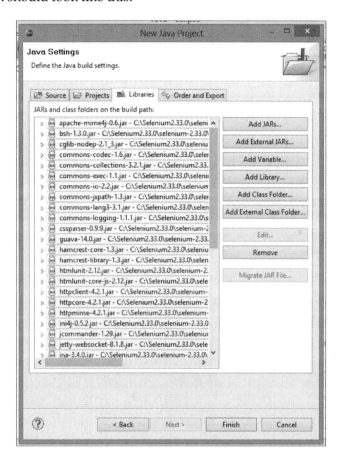

5. Click on **Finish**.

6. Now, let's create our first class that uses WebDriver to navigate to a web page. In the project explorer window of Eclipse, right-click and navigate to **src | New | Class**, enter the details of the class name and package name, as shown in the following screenshot, and then click on **Finish**:

7. The first piece of code to invoke WebDriver and navigate to a URL is as follows:

```
package com.packt.webdriver.chapter1;
import org.openqa.selenium.WebDriver;
import org.openqa.selenium.firefox.FirefoxDriver;
public class NavigateToAUrl {
    public static void main(String[] args){
        WebDriver driver = new FirefoxDriver();
        driver.get("http://www.google.com");
    }
}
```

Lets look at each line of code. Line 1 is the name of the package in which your class file is going to reside, lines 2 and 3 import necessary WebDriver classes that we are going to explore, line 4 is the class declaration, and line 5 is the start of the main method.

Now, coming to the important part of the code:

```
WebDriver driver = new FirefoxDriver();
```

Line 6 is where we instantiate the Firefox implementation of the WebDriver interface. WebDriver is an interface whose concrete implementation is done in two classes: RemoteWebDriver and HtmlUnitDriver.

We will talk about the RemoteWebDriver and HtmlUnitDriver classes more in depth later in this book, but right now knowing them as implementations of the WebDriver interface is sufficient. FirefoxDriver is a subclass of the RemoteWebDriver class, which extends the RemoteWebDriver class more specifically for the Firefox browser. Similarly, we have the InternetExplorerDriver, ChromeDriver, SafariDriver, AndroidDriver, and IPhoneDriver classes, which are specific implementations for the respective browsers and devices. The following figure shows the hierarchy of the classes:

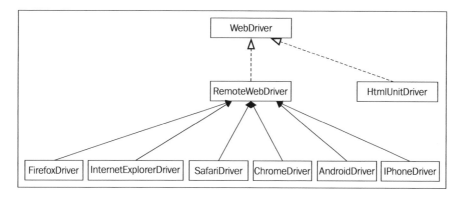

Let's now look at the last line of the code:

```
driver.get("http://www.google.com");
```

In the preceding code, we use one of the methods of the `WebDriver` interface called the `get()` method to make the browser load the requested web page on it. If the browser, in this case Firefox, is not already opened, it will launch a new browser window.

8. Now, execute your code by navigating to **Run** | **Run** or using the *Ctrl* + *F11* shortcut. A Firefox browser should open and load the Google Search page in your browser.

WebElements

A web page is comprised of many different HTML elements, such as buttons, links, a body, labels, forms, and so on, that are named WebElements in the context of WebDriver. Together, these elements on a web page will achieve the business functionality. For example, let's look at the HTML code of the login page of a website.

```html
<html>
  <body>
    <form id="loginForm">
      <label>Enter Username: </label>
      <input type="text" name="Username"/>
      <label>Enter Password: </label>
      <input type="password" name="Password"/>
      <input type="submit"/>
    </form>
    <a href="forgotPassword.html">Forgot Password ?</a>
  </body>
</html>
```

In the preceding HTML code, there are different types of WebElements such as `<html>`, `<body>`, `<form>`, `<label>`, `<input>`, and `<a>`, which together make a web page. Let's analyze the following WebElement:

```html
<label>Enter Username: </label>
```

Here, `<label>` is the start tag of the WebElement label. `Enter Username:` is the text present on the `label` element. Finally, `</label>` is the end tag, which indicates the end of WebElement.

Similarly, take another WebElement:

```html
<input type="text" name="Username"/>
```

In the preceding code, `type` and `name` are the attributes of the WebElement `input` with values `text` and `Username`, respectively.

UI Automation is mostly about locating these WebElements on a web page and executing user actions on them. In the rest of the chapter, we will use various ways to locate WebElements and execute relevant user actions on them.

Locating WebElements using WebDriver

Let's start this section by automating the Google Search page, which involves opening the Google Search page, typing the search text in the textbox, and executing the search. The code for that is as follows:

```
public class GoogleSearch {
  public static void main(String[] args){
    WebDriver driver = new FirefoxDriver();
    driver.get("http://www.google.com");
    WebElement searchBox = driver.findElement(By.name("q"));
    searchBox.sendKeys("Packt Publishing");
    searchBox.submit();
  }
}
```

In the preceding code, lines 1 to 4 are same as the example discussed earlier. When you look at line 5, there are three new things that are highlighted as follows:

```
WebElement searchBox = driver.findElement(By.name("q"));
```

They are the findElement() method, By.name() method, and the WebElement interface. The findElement() and By() methods instruct WebDriver to locate a WebElement on a web page, and once found, the findElement() method returns the WebElement instance of that element. Actions such as click, type, and so on, are performed on a returned WebElement using the methods declared in the WebElement interface, which will be discussed in detail in the next section.

The findElement() method

In UI automation, locating an element is the first step before executing any user actions on it. WebDriver's findElement() method is a convenient way to locate an element on the web page. According to WebDriver's Javadoc (http://selenium.googlecode.com/git/docs/api/java/index.html), the method declaration is as follows:

```
WebElement findElement(By by)
```

So, the input parameter for the findElement() method is the By instance. The By instance is a WebElement-locating mechanism. There are eight different ways to locate a WebElement on a web page. We will see that when we discuss By, shortly.

The return type of the findElement() method is the WebElement instance that represents the actual HTML element or component of the web page. The method returns the first WebElement that the driver comes across which satisfies the locating-mechanism condition. This WebElement instance will act as a handle to that component from then on. Appropriate actions can be taken on that component by the test script developer using this returned WebElement instance.

If WebDriver doesn't find the element, it throws a runtime exception named NoSuchElementException, which the invoking class or method should handle. The test script developer is advised to avoid using this method if he/she thinks the WebElement will not be present on the web page. For those purposes, we can use another method of WebDriver named findElements.

The findElements() method

If developers think that they may encounter zero or more number of WebElements for a given locating mechanism on a web page, they should rather use the findElements() method than the findElement() method. Because the findElement() method throws NoSuchElementException in case of zero occurrences of WebElement and on the other hand, only the first occurred WebElement that satisfies the locating mechanism condition though the web page contains multiple WebElements. The method declaration of the findElements() method is as follows:

```
java.util.List<WebElement> findElements(By by)
```

The input parameter is same as the findElement() method, which is an instance of the By class. The difference lies in the return type. Here, if no element is found, an empty list is returned and if there are multiple WebElements present satisfying the locating mechanism, all of them are returned to the caller in a list.

Firebug

Before we discuss about locating mechanism using the By class, we have to see how Firebug works. Firebug is an add-on/plugin for Firefox, which we have installed earlier. This is used to inspect the HTML elements on a web page loaded in Firefox. Let's load www.google.com on Firefox. To inspect the search button element, launch the firebug plugin by clicking on the firebug icon close to the top-right corner, as shown in the following screenshot:

Once launched, click on the **Inspect Element** icon, which looks like the following screenshot:

Now move the cursor to the search button element and click on it. Firebug will highlight the HTML code that represents the element on the web page. In this case, it will be:

```
<button class="gbqfba" name="btnK" aria-label="Google Search"
id="gbqfba"><span id="gbqfsa">Google Search</span></button>
```

As Firebug shows the respective HTML code for the WebElement, now it's the developer's choice to select the attribute of the element used to locate the element and pass it to the `findElement()` method. For example, in this case, the element has `name`, `class`, and `id` attributes declared. So it is up to the developer to choose one attribute of the WebElement to identify the element uniquely.

 WebElements on a web page may not have all the attributes declared. It is up to the developer of the test script to select the attribute that uniquely identifies the WebElement on the web page for the automation.

Using the By locating mechanism

`By` is the locating mechanism passed to the `findElement()` method or the `findElements()` method to fetch the respective WebElement(s) on a web page. There are eight different locating mechanisms; that is, eight different ways to identify an HTML element on a web page. They are located by Name, ID, TagName, Class, LinkText, PartialLinkText, XPath, and CSS.

The By.name() method

As seen earlier, every element on a web page has many attributes. Name is one among them. For instance, the HTML code for the **Google Search** button will be:

```
<button id="gbqfba" aria-label="Google Search" name="btnK"
class="gbqfba"><span id="gbqfsa">Google Search</span></button>
```

Here name is one of the many attributes of the button, and its value is btnK. If we want to identify this button and click on it in your test script, the code will look as follows:

```
public class GoogleSearchButtonByName {
  public static void main(String[] args){
    WebDriver driver = new FirefoxDriver();
    driver.get("http://www.google.com");
    WebElement searchBox = driver.findElement(By.name("btnK"));
    searchBox.submit();
  }
}
```

If you observe line 5, the locating mechanism used here is By.name and the name is btnK. So, from where did we get this name? As discussed in the previous section, it is the firebug that helped us get the name of the button. Launch the Firebug and use the inspect elements widget to get the attributes of an element.

The By.id() method

On a web page, each element is uniquely identified by an ID, if provided. An ID can be assigned manually by the developer of the web application or, most of the times, left to be dynamically generated by the server where the web application is hosted, and this ID can change over a period of time.

Now, if we consider the same HTML code of the **Google Search** button:

```
<button id="gbqfba" aria-label="Google Search" name="btnK"
class="gbqfba"><span id="gbqfsa">Google Search</span></button>
```

In the preceding code, the id value of this button is gbqfba. This might change by the time you read this book, because this could be a server-generated ID.

Let us see what changes need to be made to our test script to use id instead of name:

```
public class GoogleSearchButtonById {
  public static void main(String[] args){
    WebDriver driver = new FirefoxDriver();
    driver.get("http://www.google.com");
    WebElement searchBox = driver.findElement(By.id("gbqfba"));
    searchBox.submit();
  }
}
```

We have changed the locating mechanism from the `By.name()` method to the `By.id()` method, and used the search button's `id` value instead of `name`. Here, try to use the `By.id` identifier, and use the `name` value (that is. `btnK`) instead of the `id` value (that is. `gbqfba`). Modify line 5 as follows:

```
WebElement searchBox = driver.findElement(By.id("btnK"));
```

The test script will fail to throw an exception as follows:

```
Exception in thread "main" org.openqa.selenium.NoSuchElementException:
Unable to locate element: {"method":"id","selector":"btnK"}
```

WebDriver couldn't find an element by `id` whose value is `btnK`. Thus, it throws an exception saying it couldn't find any such element with `id` as `btnK`.

The By.tagName() method

Locating an element by tag name is slightly different from `name` and `id` locating mechanisms. The reason being it can return zero or more results. For example, on a Google Search page, if you search for an element with the tag name button, it will result in three WebElements because there are three buttons present on the search page. So it is always advisable to use the `findElements()` method rather than the `findElement()` method when trying to locate elements using tag names.

Let's see how the code looks like when a search for the number of buttons present on a Google Search page is made.

```
public class GoogleSearchPageByTagName{
  public static void main(String[] args){
    WebDriver driver = new FirefoxDriver();
    driver.get("http://www.google.com");
    List<WebElement> buttons =   driver.findElements(By.
tagName("button"));
    System.out.println(buttons.size());
  }
}
```

In the preceding code, we have used the `By.tagName` locating mechanism and `findElements()` method, which returns a list of all the buttons available on the page. On line 6, when we printed the size of the list, it returns 3.

If you are wondering how there are three buttons on the Google Search page while only two are visible, the following are all the buttons available on the search page:

```
<button id=gbqfb aria-label="Google Search" class=gbqfb
name=btnG><span class=gbqfi></span></button>
<button id=gbqfba aria-label="Google Search" name=btnK
class=gbqfba><span id=gbqfsa>Google Search</span></button>
```

```
<button id=gbqfbb aria-label="I'm Feeling Lucky" name=btnI
class=gbqfba onclick="if(this.form.q.value)this.checked=1;else window.
top.location='/doodles/'"><span id=gbqfsb>I'm Feeling Lucky</span></
button>
```

This is why WebDriver is so helpful to reveal things that are difficult to figure out manually.

Some commonly used HTML elements are mentioned as follows, and they can be used by tag names (also mentioned).

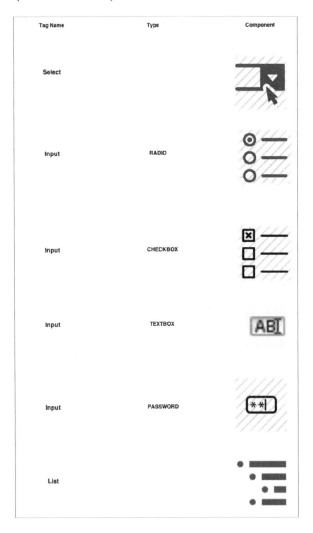

Tag Name	Type	Component
Select		
Input	RADIO	
Input	CHECKBOX	
Input	TEXTBOX	
Input	PASSWORD	
List		

There are many tags whose names are input. For those, you have to further filter them by using the `type` attribute. We will learn that in the next section.

The By.className() method

Before we discuss about the `className()` method, we have to talk a little about style and CSS. Every HTML element on a web page, generally, is styled by the web page developer or designer. It is not mandatory that each element should be styled, but it is generally followed to make it appealing to the end user.

So, in order to apply styles to an element, they can be declared directly in the element tag or placed in a separate file called the CSS file and can be referenced in the element using the `className()` method. For instance, a `style` attribute for a button can be declared in a CSS file as follows:

```
.buttonStyle{
    width: 50px;
    height: 50px;
    border-radius: 50%;
    margin: 0% 2%;
}
```

Now, this style can be applied on the button element in a web page as follows:

```
<button name="sampleBtnName" id="sampleBtnId" class="buttonStyle">I'm
Button</button>
```

So, `buttonStyle` is used as value for the `class` attribute of the button element, and it inherits all the styles declared in the CSS file. Now, let's try this on our Google search page. We will try to make WebDriver identify the search box using its class name and type some text into it. First, in order to get the class name of the search box, as we know, we will use Firebug and fetch it. After getting it, change the location mechanism to `By.className` and specify the `class` attribute value in it. The code for that is as follows:

```
public class GoogleSearchByClassName{
  public static void main(String[] args){
    WebDriver driver = new FirefoxDriver();
    driver.get("http://www.google.com");
    WebElement searchBox = driver.findElement(By.className("gbqfif"));
    searchBox.sendKeys("Packt Publishing");
  }
}
```

In the preceding code, we have used the `By.className` locating mechanism by passing the `class` attribute value to it.

The By.linkText() method

As the name suggests, the By.linkText locating mechanism can only be used to identify the HTML links. Before we start discussing about how WebDriver can be commanded to identify a link element using link text, let's see what an HTML link element looks like. The HTML link elements are represented on a web page using the <a> tag, abbreviation for the anchor tag. A typical anchor tag looks like this:

```
<a href="/intl/en/about.html">About Google</a>
```

Here, href is the link to a different page where your web browser will take you when clicked on the link. So, the preceding HTML code when rendered by the browser looks like this:

About Google

This **About Google** is the link text. So the locating mechanism By.linkText uses this text on an anchor tag to identify the WebElement. The code for this would look like this:

```
public class GoogleSearchByLinkText{
  public static void main(String[] args){
    WebDriver driver = new FirefoxDriver();
    driver.get("http://www.google.com");
    WebElement aboutLink = driver.findElement(By.linkText("About
Google"));
    aboutLink.click();
  }
}
```

Here, the By.linkText locating mechanism is used to identify the **About Google** link.

The By.partialLinkText() method

The By.partialLinkText locating mechanism is an extension to the previous one. If you are not sure of the entire link text or want to use only part of the link text, you can use this locating mechanism to identify the link element. So let's modify the previous example to use only partial text on the link, that is, **About**.

```
public class GoogleSearchByPartialLinkText{
  public static void main(String[] args){
    WebDriver driver = new FirefoxDriver();
    driver.get("http://www.google.com");
```

```
    WebElement aboutLink = driver.findElement(By.
partialLinkText("About"));
        aboutLink.click();
    }
}
```

What happens if there are multiple links whose text has **About** in it? That is a question to the `findElement()` method rather than to the locating mechanism. Remember when we discussed the `findElement()` method earlier, it will return only the first WebElement that it comes across. If you want all the WebElements which contain **About** in its link text, use the `findElements()` method, which will return a list of all those elements.

> Use WebDriver's `findElements()` method if you think you need all the WebElements that satisfy a locating mechanism condition.

The By.xpath() method

WebDriver uses **XPath** to identify a WebElement on the web page. Before we see how it does that, we will quickly look at the syntax for XPath. XPath is a short name for the XML path. The HTML for our web page is also one form of the XML document. So in order to identify an element on an HTML page, we need to use a specific XPath syntax as follows:

- The root element is identified as `//`
- To identify all the `div` elements, the syntax will be `//div`
- To identify the `link` tags that are within the `div` element, the syntax will be `//div/a`
- To identify all the elements with a tag, we use `*`. The syntax will be `//div/*`
- To identify all the `div` elements that are at three levels down from the root, we can use `//*/*/div`
- To identify specific elements, we use attribute values of those elements, such as `//*/div/a[@id='attrValue']`, which will return the `anchor` element. This element is at third level from root within a `div` element, and has an `id` value `attrValue`

So, we need to pass these kinds of XPath syntaxes to our WebDriver to make it identify our target element. But going through the HTML page figuring out the XPath for each element will be extremely difficult. For this, if you remember, we have installed a Firebug extension named FirePath. This will quickly give you the XPath of the target element that you can use in the WebDriver code. Following is the screenshot of the XPath of the **Google Search** button:

If you see the preceding image, the **Google Search** Button is selected and in the **FirePath** tab below the XPath, the value is displayed as *//*[@id='gbqfba']*.

Now, let us see the code example and how WebDriver uses this XPath to identify the element.

```
public class GoogleSearchByXPath{
  public static void main(String[] args){
    WebDriver driver = new FirefoxDriver();
    driver.get("http://www.google.com");
    WebElement searchButton =  driver.findElement(By.xpath("//*[@
id='gbqfba']"));
    System.out.println(searchButton.getText());
  }
}
```

In the preceding code, we are using the By.xpath locating mechanism and passing the XPath of the WebElement to it.

One disadvantage of using XPath is it is costly in terms of time. For every element to be identified, WebDriver actually scans through the entire page that is very time consuming, and too much usage of XPath in your test script will actually make them too slow to be executed.

The By.cssSelector() method

The `By.cssSelector()` method is similar to the `By.xpath()` method in its usage but the difference is that it is slightly faster than the `By.xpath` locating mechanism. Following are the commonly used syntaxes to identify elements:

- To identify an element using the `div` element with `id` `#flrs`, we use the `#flrs` syntax

- To identify the child `anchor` element, we use the `#flrs > a` syntax, which will return the `link` element

- To identify the `anchor` element with its attribute, we use the `#flrs > a[a[href="/intl/en/about.html"]]` syntax

Let's try to modify the previous code, which uses the XPath-locating mechanism to use the `cssSelector` mechanism.

```
public class GoogleSearchByCSSSelector{
  public static void main(String[] args){
    WebDriver driver = new FirefoxDriver();
    driver.get("http://www.google.com");
    WebElement searchButton = driver.findElement(By.
cssSelector("#gbqfba"));
    System.out.println(searchButton.getText());
  }
}
```

The preceding code uses the `By.cssSelector` locating mechanism that uses the css selector ID of the **Google Search** button.

Let's look at a slightly complex example. We will try to identify the **About Google** link on the Google Search page:

```
public class GoogleSearchByCSSSelector{
  public static void main(String[] args){
    WebDriver driver = new FirefoxDriver();
    driver.get("http://www.google.com");
    WebElement searchButton = driver.findElement(By.
cssSelector("#flrs>a[href='/intl/en/about.html']"));
    System.out.println(searchButton.getText());
  }
}
```

The preceding code uses the `cssSelector()` method to find the `anchor` element identified by its `href` attribute [ ].

Actions on WebElements

In the previous section, we have seen how to locate WebElements on a web page by using different locating mechanisms. Here, we will see all the different user actions that can be taken on a WebElement. Different WebElements will have different actions that can be taken on them. For example, in a textbox element, we can type in some text or clear the text that is already typed in it. Similarly for a button, we can click on it, get the dimensions of it, and so on, but we cannot type into a button, and for a link, we cannot type into it. So, though all the actions are listed in one WebElement interface, it is the test script developer's responsibility to use the actions that are supported by the target element. In case we try to execute a wrong action on a WebElement, we don't see any exception or error thrown and also we don't see any action that really gets executed; WebDriver ignores such actions silently.

Now, let's get into each of the actions individually by looking into their Javadocs and a code example.

The getAttribute() method

The `getAttribute` action can be executed on all the WebElements. Remember we have seen attributes of WebElement in the WebElements section. The HTML attributes are modifiers of HTML elements. They are generally key-value pairs appearing in the start tag of an element. For example, in the following WebElement:

```
<label name="Username" id="uname">Enter Username: </label>
```

In the preceding code, `name` and `id` are the attributes or attribute keys and `Username` and `uname` are the attribute values.

The API syntax of the `getAttributes()` method is as follows:

```
java.lang.String getAttribute(java.lang.String name)
```

In the preceding code, the input parameter is `String`, which is the name of the attribute. The return type is again `String`, which is the value of the attribute.

Now let's see how we can get all the attributes of a WebElement using WebDriver. Here, we will make use of the **Google Search** button again. This is what the element looks like:

```
<button id="gbqfba" class="gbqfba" name="btnK" aria-label="Google
Search">
```

We will list all the attributes of this WebElement using WebDriver. The code for that is as follows:

```
public class GetAttributes{
  public static void main(String[] args){
    WebDriver driver = new FirefoxDriver();
    driver.get("http://www.google.com");
    WebElement searchButton = driver.findElement(By.name("btnK"));
    System.out.println("Name of the button is: "
                            +searchButton.getAttribute("name"));
    System.out.println("Id of the button is: "
+searchButton.getAttribute("id"));
    System.out.println("Class of the button is: "
                            +searchButton.getAttribute("class"));
    System.out.println("Label of the button is: "
                            +searchButton.getAttribute("aria-  label"));
  }
}
```

In the preceding code, the last four lines of code use the getAttribute() method to fetch the attribute values of the attribute name, id, class, and aria-label of the **Google Search** button WebElement. The output of the preceding code is shown in the following screenshot:

```
Name of the button is: btnK
Id of the button is: gbqfba
Class of the button is: gbqfba
Label of the button is: null
```

Going back to the By.tagName() method of the previous section, if the search by locating mechanism, By.tagName, results in more than one result, you can use the getAttribute() method to further filter the results and get to your exact intended element.

The sendKeys() method

The sendKeys action is applicable for textbox or textarea HTML elements. This is used to type text into the textbox. This will simulate the user keyboard and types text into WebElements exactly as would a user.

The API syntax for the sendKeys() method is as follows:

```
void sendKeys(java.lang.CharSequence...keysToSend)
```

The input parameter for the preceding method is `CharSequence` of text that has to be entered into the element. This method doesn't return anything.

Now, let's see a code example of how to type a search text into the **Google Search** box using the `sendKeys()` method.

```
public class sendKeys{
  public static void main(String[] args){
    WebDriver driver = new FirefoxDriver();
    driver.get("http://www.google.com");
    WebElement searchBox = driver.findElement(By.name("q"));
    searchButton.sendKeys("Packt Publishing");
  }
}
```

In the preceding code, the `sendKeys()` method is used to type the required text in the textbox element of the web page. This is how we deal with normal keys, but if you want to type in some special keys, such as *Backspace, Enter, Tab, Shift*, and so on, we need to use a special `enum` class of WebDriver named `Keys`. Using the `Keys` enumeration, you can simulate many special keys while typing into a WebElement. Now let's see some code example, which uses the *Shift* key to type the text in uppercase in the **Google Search** Box:

```
public class SendKeys{
  public static void main(String[] args){
    WebDriver driver = new FirefoxDriver();
    driver.get("http://www.google.com");
    WebElement searchBox = driver.findElement(By.name("q"));
    searchBox.sendKeys(Keys.chord(Keys.SHIFT,"packt publishing"));
  }
}
```

In the preceding code, the `chord()` method from the `Keys` enum is used to type the key while the text specified is being given as an input to be the textbox. Try this in your environment to see all the text being typed in uppercase.

The clear() method

The `clear` action is similar to the `sendKeys()` method, which is applicable for textbox and textarea elements. This is used to erase the text that is entered in a WebElement using the `sendKeys()` method. This can be achieved using the `Keys.BACK_SPACE` enum, but WebDriver has given us an explicit method to clear the text easily.

The API syntax for the `clear()` method is as follows:

```
void clear()
```

This method doesn't take any input and doesn't return any output. It is simply executed on the target text entry element.

Now, let us see how we can clear text that is entered in the **Google Search** box. The code example for it is as follows:

```
public class Clear{
  public static void main(String[] args){
    WebDriver driver = new FirefoxDriver();
    driver.get("http://www.google.com");
    WebElement searchBox = driver.findElement(By.name("q"));
    searchBox.sendKeys(Keys.chord(Keys.SHIFT,"packt publishing"));
    searchBox.clear();
  }
}
```

We have used the WebElement's `clear()` method to clear the text after typing `packt publishing` into the **Google Search** box.

The submit() method

The `submit` action can be taken on a form or on an element, which is inside a form. This is used to submit a form of a web page to the server hosting the web application.

The API syntax for the `submit()` method is as follows:

```
void submit()
```

The preceding method doesn't take any input parameter and doesn't return anything. But a `NoSuchElementException` is thrown when this method is executed on a WebElement that is not present within a form.

Now, let's see a code example to submit the form on a Google Search page:

```
public class Submit{
  public static void main(String[] args){
    WebDriver driver = new FirefoxDriver();
    driver.get("http://www.google.com");
    WebElement searchBox = driver.findElement(By.name("q"));
    searchBox.sendKeys(Keys.chord(Keys.SHIFT,"packt publishing"));
    searchBox.submit();
  }
}
```

In the preceding code, towards the end is where the Search form is submitted to the Google servers using the submit() method. Now, try to execute the submit() method on an element, let's say the **About Google** link, which is not a part of any form. We should see a NoSuchElementException being thrown.

So when you use the submit() method on a WebElement, make sure it is part of the form element.

The getCssValue() method

The getCssValue action can be taken on all the WebElements. This is used to fetch the CSS properties' values of the given element. CSS properties can be font-family, background-color, color, and so on. This is useful when you want to validate the CSS styles that are applied to your WebElements through your test scripts.

The API syntax for the getCssValue() method is as follows:

```
java.lang.String getCssValue(java.lang.String propertyName)
```

In the preceding code, the input parameter is the String value of the CSS property name, and return type is the value assigned for that property name.

The following is the code example to retrieve the font-family of the text on the **Google Search** button:

```
public class GetCSSValue{
  public static void main(String[] args){
    WebDriver driver = new FirefoxDriver();
    driver.get("http://www.google.com");
    WebElement searchButton = driver.findElement(By.name("btnK"));
    System.out.println(searchButton.getCssValue("font-family"));
  }
}
```

The preceding code uses the getCssValue() method to find the font-family of the text visible on the **Google Search** button. The output of this is shown in the following screenshot:

Similarly, we can retrieve the background color of an element using this method. Let us see a code for this:

```
public class GetCSSValue2{
  public static void main(String[] args){
    WebDriver driver = new FirefoxDriver();
   driver.get("http://www.google.com");
    WebElement searchButton = driver.findElement(By.name("btnK"));
    System.out.println(searchButton.getCssValue("background-color"));
  }
}
```

The output for the preceding code is shown in the following screenshot:

The getLocation() method

The `getLocation` action can be executed on all the WebElements. This is used to get the relative position of an element where it is rendered on the web page. This position is calculated relative to the top-left corner of the web page of which the (x, y) coordinates are assumed as (0, 0). This method will be of use if your test script tries to validate the layout of your web page.

The API syntax of the `getLocation()` method is as follows:

```
Point getLocation()
```

The preceding method obviously doesn't take any input parameter, but the return type is a `Point` class, which contains the (x, y) coordinates of the element.

The following is the code to retrieve the location of the **Google Search** button:

```
public class GetLocation{
  public static void main(String[] args){
    WebDriver driver = new FirefoxDriver();
    driver.get("http://www.google.com");
    WebElement searchButton = driver.findElement(By.name("btnK"));
    System.out.println(searchButton.getLocation());
  }
}
```

The output for the preceding code is the (x, y) location of the **Google Search** button, as shown in the following screenshot:

The getSize() method

The getSize action can also be applied on all the visible components of HTML. It will return the width and height of the rendered WebElement.

The API syntax of the getSize() method is as follows:

```
Dimension getSize()
```

The preceding method doesn't take any input parameters, and the return type is a class instance named Dimension. This class contains the width and height of the target WebElement.

The following is the code to get the width and height of our favorite **Google Search** button:

```
public class GetSize{
public static void main(String[] args){
  WebDriver driver = new FirefoxDriver();
  driver.get("http://www.google.com");
  WebElement searchButton = driver.findElement(By.name("btnK"));
  System.out.println(searchButton.getSize());
  }
}
```

The output for the preceding code is the width and height of the **Google Search** button, as shown in the following screenshot:

The getText() method

The getText action can be taken on all the WebElements. It will give the visible text if the element contains any text on it or else will return nothing.

The API syntax for the getText() method is as follows:

```
java.lang.String getText()
```

There is no input parameter for the preceding method, but it returns the visible innerText string of the WebElement if anything is available, else will return an empty string.

The following is the code to get the text present on the **Google Search** button:

```
public class GetText{
  public static void main(String[] args){
    WebDriver driver = new FirefoxDriver();
    driver.get("http://www.google.com");
    WebElement searchButton = driver.findElement(By.name("btnK"));
    System.out.println(searchButton.getText());
  }
}
```

The preceding code uses the getText() method to fetch the text present on the **Google Search** button, which returns the following:

The getTagName() method

The getTagName action can be taken on all the WebElements. This will return the tag name of the WebElement. For example, in the following HTML code, button is the tag name of the HTML element:

```
<button id="gbqfba" class="gbqfba" name="btnK" aria-label="Google
Search">
```

In the preceding code, button is the tag name of the HTML element.

The API syntax for the getTagName() method is as follows:

```
java.lang.String getTagName()
```

The return type of the preceding method is String, and it returns the tag name of the target element.

The following is the code that returns the tag name of the **Google Search** button:

```
public class GetTagName{
  public static void main(String[] args){
    WebDriver driver = new FirefoxDriver();
    driver.get("http://www.google.com");
    WebElement searchButton = driver.findElement(By.name("btnK"));
    System.out.println(searchButton.getTagName());
  }
}
```

The preceding code uses the `getTagName()` method to get the tag name of the **Google Search** button element. The output of the code is as expected:

The isDisplayed() method

The `isDisplayed` action verifies if an element is displayed on the web page and can be executed on all the WebElements.

The API syntax for the `isDisplayed()` method is as follows:

```
boolean isDisplayed()
```

The preceding method returns a Boolean value specifying whether the target element is displayed or not displayed on the web page.

The following is the code to verify if the **Google Search** button is displayed or not, which obviously should return `true` in this case:

```
public class isDisplayed{
  public static void main(String[] args){
    WebDriver driver = new FirefoxDriver();
    driver.get("http://www.google.com");
    WebElement searchButton = driver.findElement(By.name("btnK"));
    System.out.println(searchButton.isDisplayed());
  }
}
```

The preceding code uses the `isDisplayed()` method to determine if the element is displayed on a web page. The preceding code returns `true` for the **Google Search** button.

The isEnabled() method

The `isEnabled` action verifies if an element is enabled on the web page and can be executed on all the WebElements.

The API syntax for the `isEnabled()` method is as follows:

```
boolean isEnabled()
```

The preceding method returns a Boolean value specifying whether the target element is enabled or not enabled on the web page.

The following is the code to verify if the **Google Search** button is enabled or not, which obviously should return `true` in this case:

```
public class isEnabled{
  public static void main(String[] args){
    WebDriver driver = new FirefoxDriver();
    driver.get("http://www.google.com");
    WebElement searchButton = driver.findElement(By.name("btnK"));
    System.out.println(searchButton.isEnabled());
  }
}
```

The preceding code uses the `isEnabled()` method to determine if the element is displayed on a web page. The preceding code returns true for the **Google Search** button.

The isSelected() method

The `isSelected` action verifies if an element is selected right now on the web page and can be executed only on a radio button, options in select, and checkbox WebElements. When executed on other elements, it will return `false`.

The API syntax for the `isSelected()` method is as follows:

```
boolean isSelected()
```

The preceding method returns a Boolean value specifying whether the target element is selected or not selected on the web page.

The following is the code to verify if the **Google Search** box is selected or not on a search page:

```java
public class IsSelected{
  public static void main(String[] args){
    WebDriver driver = new FirefoxDriver();
    driver.get("http://www.google.com");
    WebElement searchBox = driver.findElement(By.name("q"));
    System.out.println(searchBox.isSelected());
  }
}
```

The preceding code uses the `isSelected()` method. It returns `false` for the **Google Search** box, because this is not a radio button, options in select, or a checkbox.

Summary

In this chapter, we have seen a brief history of Selenium, the architecture of WebDriver, WebElements, how to locate them, and actions that can be taken on them. We have also covered some of the fundamentals of WebDriver, which are useful in your day-to-day dealing with WebDriver.

In the next chapter, we will see more advanced actions that can be performed on WebElements.

2
Exploring Advanced Interactions of WebDriver

In the previous chapter, we have discussed WebElements, how to locate them on a web page, and some basic actions that can be performed on them. In this chapter, we will go through some advanced ways of performing actions on WebElements.

Understanding actions, build, and perform

We know how to take some basic actions, such as clicking on a button and typing text into a textbox; however, there are many scenarios where we have to perform multiple actions at the same time. For example, keeping the *Shift* button pressed and typing text for uppercase letters, and the dragging and dropping mouse actions.

Let's see a simple scenario here. Open the `selectable.html` file that is attached with this book. You will see tiles of numbers from **1** to **12**. If you inspect the elements with Firebug, you will see an ordered list tag (`<ol>`) and 12 list items (`<li>`) under it, as shown in the following code:

```
<ol id="selectable" class="ui-selectable">
<li class="ui-state-default ui-selectee" name="one">1</li>
<li class="ui-state-default ui-selectee" name="two">2</li>
<li class="ui-state-default ui-selectee" name="three">3</li>
<li class="ui-state-default ui-selectee" name="four">4</li>
<li class="ui-state-default ui-selectee" name="five">5</li>
<li class="ui-state-default ui-selectee" name="six">6</li>
<li class="ui-state-default ui-selectee" name="seven">7</li>
<li class="ui-state-default ui-selectee" name="eight">8</li>
<li class="ui-state-default ui-selectee" name="nine">9</li>
<li class="ui-state-default ui-selectee" name="ten">10</li>
```

```
<li class="ui-state-default ui-selectee" name="eleven">11</li>
<li class="ui-state-default ui-selectee" name="twelve">12</li>
</ol>
```

If you click a number, it's background color changes to orange. Try selecting the **1**, **3**, and **5** numbered tiles. You do that by holding the *Ctrl* key + **1** numbered tile + **3** numbered tile + **5** numbered tile. So, this involves performing multiple actions, that is, holding the *Ctrl* key continuously and clicking on **1**, **3**, and **5** tiles. How do we perform these multiple actions using WebDriver? The following code demonstrates that:

```
public class ActionBuildPerform {
    public static void main(String... args) {
      WebDriver driver = new FirefoxDriver();
      driver.get("file://C:/selectable.html");
      WebElement one = driver.findElement(By.name("one"));
      WebElement three = driver.findElement(By.name("three"));
      WebElement five = driver.findElement(By.name("five"));
      // Add all the actions into the Actions builder.
      Actions builder = new Actions(driver);
        builder.keyDown(Keys.CONTROL)
              .click(one)
            .click(three)
            .click(five)
            .keyUp(Keys.CONTROL);
      // Generate the composite action.
      Action compositeAction = builder.build();
      // Perform the composite action.
      compositeAction.perform();
      }
    }
}
```

Now, if you see the code, line number 9 is where we are getting introduced to a new class named `Actions`. This `Actions` class is the one that is used to emulate all the complex user events. Using this, the developer of the test script could combine all the necessary user gestures into one composite action. From line 9 to line 14, we have declared all the actions that are to be executed to achieve the functionality of clicking on the numbers **1**, **3**, and **5**. Once all the actions are grouped together, we build that into a composite action. This is contained on line 16. `Action` is an interface that has only the `perform()` method, which executes the composite action. Line 18 is where we are actually executing the action using the `perform()` method.

So, to make WebDriver perform multiple actions at the same time, you need to follow a three-step process of using the user-facing API of the Actions class to group all the actions, then build the composite action, and then the perform the action. This process can be made into a two-step process as the perform() method internally calls the build() method. So the previous code will look as follows:

```
public class ActionBuildPerform {
    public static void main(String... args) {
        WebDriver driver = new FirefoxDriver();
        driver.get("file://C:/selectable.html");
        WebElement one = driver.findElement(By.name("one"));
        WebElement three = driver.findElement(By.name("three"));
        WebElement five = driver.findElement(By.name("five"));
        // Add all the actions into the Actions builder.
        Actions builder = new Actions(driver);
        builder.keyDown(Keys.CONTROL)
                .click(one)
                .click(three)
                .click(five)
                .keyUp(Keys.CONTROL);
        // Perform the action.
        builder.perform();
    }
}
```

In the preceding code, we have directly invoked the perform() method on the Actions instance, which internally calls the build() method to create a composite action before executing it.

In the subsequent sections of this chapter, we will take a closer look at the Actions class. All the actions are basically divided into two categories: mouse-based actions and keyboard-based actions. In the following sections, we will discuss all the actions that are specific to the mouse and keyboard available in the Actions class.

Learning mouse-based interactions

There are around eight different mouse actions that can be performed using the Actions class. We will see each of their syntax and a working example.

The moveByOffset action

The moveByOffset() method is used to move the mouse from its current position to another point on the web page. Developers can specify the X distance and Y distance the mouse has to be moved. When the page is loaded, generally the initial position of a mouse would be (0, 0), unless there is an explicit focus declared by the page.

The API syntax for the moveByOffset() method is as follows:

```
public Actions moveByOffset(int xOffSet, int yOffSet)
```

In the preceding code, xOffSet is the input parameter providing the WebDriver the amount of offset to be moved along the x axis. A positive value is used to move the cursor to the right, and a negative value is used to move the cursor to the left.

yOffSet is the input parameter providing the WebDriver the amount of offset to be moved along the y axis. A positive value is used to move the cursor down along the y axis and a negative value is used to move the cursor toward the top.

When the xOffSet and yOffSet values result in moving the cursor out of the document, a MoveTargetOutOfBoundsException is raised.

Let's see a working example of it. The objective of the following code is to move the cursor on to the number **3** tile on the web page:

```
public class MoveByOffSet{
  public static void main(String... args) {
    WebDriver driver = new FirefoxDriver();
    driver.get("file://C:/Selectable.html");
    WebElement three = driver.findElement(By.name("three"));
    System.out.println("X coordinate: "+three.getLocation().getX()+"
Y coordinate: "+three.getLocation().getY());
    Actions builder = new Actions(driver);
    builder.moveByOffset(three.getLocation().getX()+1, three.
getLocation().getY()+1);
    builder.perform();
  }
}
```

We have added +1 to the coordinates, because if you observe the element in Firebug, we have a style border of 1 px. Border is a CSS-style attribute, which when applied to an element, will add a border of the specified color around the element with the specified amount of thickness. Though the previous code does move your mouse over tile **3**, we don't realize it because we are not doing any action there. We will see that when we use this moveByOffset() method in combination with the click() method shortly.

 The moveByOffset() method may not work in Mac OSX and may raise a JavaScript error when used independently like the previous code.

The click at current location action

The click() method is used to simulate the left-click of your mouse at its current point of location. This method doesn't really realize where or on which element it is clicking. It just blindly clicks wherever it is at that point of time. Hence, this method is used in combination with some other action rather than independently, to create a composite action.

The API syntax for the click() method is as follows:

```
public Actions click()
```

The click() method doesn't really have any context about where it is performing its action; hence, it doesn't take any input parameter.

Let's see a code example of the click() method:

```
public class MoveByOffsetAndClick{
  public static void main(String... args) {
    WebDriver driver = new FirefoxDriver();
    driver.get("file://C:/Selectable.html");
    WebElement seven = driver.findElement(By.name("seven"));
    System.out.println("X coordinate: "+seven.getLocation().getX()+" Y
coordinate: "+seven.getLocation().getY());
    Actions builder = new Actions(driver);
    builder.moveByOffset(seven.getLocation().getX()+1, seven.
getLocation().getY()+1).click();
    builder.perform();
  }
}
```

Line 8 is where we have used a combination of the moveByOffset() and click() methods to move the cursor from point (0, 0) to the point of tile 7. Because the initial position of the mouse is (0, 0), the X, Y offset provided for the moveByOffset() method is nothing but the location of the tile 7 element. Now, lets try to move the cursor from tile **1** to tile **11** and from there to tile **5** and see how the code looks. Before we get into the code, let's inspect the selectable.html page using Firebug. The following is the style of each tile:

```
#selectable li {
    float: left;
    font-size: 4em;
    height: 80px;
    text-align: center;
    width: 100px;
}
```

```
.ui-state-default, .ui-widget-content .ui-state-default, .ui-widget-
header .ui-state-default {
    background: url("images/ui-bg_glass_75_e6e6e6_1x400.png") repeat-x
scroll 50% 50% #E6E6E6;
    border: 1px solid #D3D3D3;
    color: #555555;
    font-weight: normal;
}
```

The three elements with which we are concerned for our offset movement in the preceding style code are: height, width, and the border thickness. Here, the height value is 80px, width value is 100px, and border value is 1px. Use these three factors to calculate the offset to navigate from one tile to the other. Note that the border thickness between any two tiles will result in 2 px; that is, 1 px from each tile. The following is the code that uses the moveByOffset and click() methods to navigate from tile **1** to tile **11**, and from there to tile **5**:

```
public class MoveByOffsetAndClick{
  public static void main(String... args) {
    WebDriver driver = new FirefoxDriver();
    driver.get("file://C:/Selectable.html");
    WebElement one = driver.findElement(By.name("one"));
    WebElement eleven = driver.findElement(By.name("eleven"));
    WebElement five = driver.findElement(By.name("five"));
    int border = 1;
    int tileWidth = 100;
    int tileHeight = 80;
    Actions builder = new Actions(driver);
    //Click on One
    builder.moveByOffset(one.getLocation().getX()+border, one.
getLocation().getY()+border).click();
    builder.build().perform();
    // Click on Eleven
    builder.moveByOffset(2*tileWidth+4*border, 2*tileHeight+4*border).
click();
    builder.build().perform();
    //Click on Five
    builder.moveByOffset(-2*tileWidth-4*border,-tileHeight-2*border).
click();
    builder.build().perform();
  }
}
```

The click on a WebElement action

We have seen how to click a WebElement by calculating the offset to it. This process may not be needed every time, especially when the WebElement has its own identifiers, such as a name or ID. We can use another overloaded version of the `click()` method to click directly on the WebElement.

The API syntax for clicking on a WebElement is as follows:

```
public Actions click(WebElement onElement)
```

The input parameter for this method is an instance of the WebElement on which the `click` action should be performed. This method, like all the other methods in the `Actions` class, will return an `Actions` instance.

Now, let's try to modify the previous code example to use the `click(WebElement)` method instead of using the `moveByOffset()` method to move to the location of the WebElement and clicking on it using the `click()` method:

```
public class ClickOnWebElement{
  public static void main(String... args) {
    WebDriver driver = new FirefoxDriver();
    driver.get("file://C:/Selectable.html");
    WebElement one = driver.findElement(By.name("one"));
    WebElement eleven = driver.findElement(By.name("eleven"));
    WebElement five = driver.findElement(By.name("five"));
    Actions builder = new Actions(driver);
    //Click on One
    builder.click(one);
    builder.build().perform();
    // Click on Eleven
    builder.click(eleven);
    builder.build().perform();
    //Click on Five
    builder.click(five)
    builder.build().perform();
  }
}
```

Now the `moveByOffset()` method has been replaced by the `click(WebElement)` method, and all of a sudden the complex coordinate geometry has been removed from the code. If you're a tester, this is one more good reason to push your developers to provide identifiers for the WebElements.

If you observe the previous code or the `moveByOffset` and `click` class code, all the operations of moving the mouse and clicking on `one`, `eleven`, and `five` tiles are built separately and performed separately. This is not how we use our `Actions` class. You can actually build all these actions together and then perform them. So, the preceding code will turn out to be as follows:

```
public class ClickOnWebElement{
  public static void main(String... args) {
    WebDriver driver = new FirefoxDriver();
    driver.get("file://C:/Selectable.html");
    WebElement one = driver.findElement(By.name("one"));
    WebElement eleven = driver.findElement(By.name("eleven"));
    WebElement five = driver.findElement(By.name("five"));
    Actions builder = new Actions(driver);
    //Click on One, Eleven and Five
    builder.click(one).click(eleven).click(five);
    builder.build().perform();
  }
}
```

The clickAndHold at current location action

The `clickAndHold()` method is another method of the `Actions` class that left-clicks on an element and holds it without releasing the left button of the mouse. This method will be useful when executing operations such as drag-and-drop. This method is one of the variants of the `clickAndHold()` method that the `Actions` class provides. We will discuss the other variant in the next section.

Now, open the `Sortable.html` file that came with the book. You can see that the tiles can be moved from one position to the other. Now let's try to move tile **3** to the position of tile **2**. The sequence of steps that are involved to do this are:

1. Move the cursor to the position of tile **3**.
2. Click and hold tile **3**.
3. Move the cursor in this position to the tile **2** location.

Now, let's see how this can be accomplished using the WebDriver's `clickAndHold()` method:

```
public class ClickAndHold{
  public static void main(String... args) {
    WebDriver driver = new FirefoxDriver();
    driver.get("file://C:/Sortable.html");
    Actions builder = new Actions(driver);
```

```
//Move tile3 to the position of tile2
builder.moveByOffset(200, 20)
        .clickAndHold()
        .moveByOffset(120, 0)
        .perform();
    }
}
```

Let's analyze the following line of code:

```
builder.moveByOffset(200, 20)
        .clickAndHold()
        .moveByOffset(120, 0)
        .perform();
```

First we move the cursor to the location of tile **3**. Then we click and hold tile **3**. Then, we move the cursor by `120px` horizontally to the position of tile **2**. The last line performs all the preceding actions. Now, execute this in your eclipse and see what happens. If you observe closely, our tile **3** doesn't properly go into the position of tile **2**. This is because we are yet to release the left button. We just commanded the WebDriver to click and hold, but not to release. Yes, in a short while, we will discuss the `release()` method of WebDriver.

The clickAndHold a WebElement action

In the previous section, we have seen the `clickAndHold()` method, which will click and hold a WebElement at the current position of the cursor. It doesn't care with which element it is dealing with. So, if we want to deal with a particular WebElement on the web page, we have to first move the cursor to the appropriate position and then perform the `clickAndHold()` action. In order to avoid the hassle of moving the cursor geometrically, WebDriver provides the developers with another variant or overloaded method of the `clickAndHold()` method that takes the WebElement as input.

The API syntax is as follows:

```
public Actions clickAndHold(WebElement onElement)
```

The input parameter for this method is the WebElement that has to be clicked and held. The return type, as in all the other methods of the `Actions` class, is the `Actions` instance.

Now, let's refactor the example in the previous section to use this method, as follows:

```
public class ClickAndHold{
  public static void main(String... args) {
    WebDriver driver = new FirefoxDriver();
```

```
driver.get("file://C:/Sortable.html");
WebElement three = driver.findElement(By.name("three"));
Actions builder = new Actions(driver);
//Move tile3 to the position of tile2
builder.clickAndHold(three)
        .moveByOffset(120, 0)
        .perform();
  }
}
```

The only change is that we have removed the action of moving the cursor to the (200, 20) position and provided the WebElement to the `clickAndHold()` method that will take care of identifying the WebElement.

The release at current location action

Now in the previous example, we have seen how to click and hold an element. The ultimate action that has to be taken on a held WebElement is to release it so that the element can be dropped or released from the mouse. The `release()` method is the one that can release the left mouse button on a WebElement.

The API syntax for the `release()` method is as follows:

```
public Actions release()
```

The preceding method doesn't take any input parameter and returns the `Actions` class instance.

Now, let's modify the previous code to include `release` action in it:

```
public class ClickAndHoldAndRelease{
  public static void main(String... args) {
    WebDriver driver = new FirefoxDriver();
    driver.get("file://C:/Sortable.html");
    WebElement three = driver.findElement(By.name("three"));
    Actions builder = new Actions(driver);
    //Move tile3 to the position of tile2
    builder.clickAndHold(three)
            .moveByOffset(120, 0)
            .release()
            .perform();
  }
}
```

The preceding code will make sure that the mouse is released at the specified location.

The release on another WebElement action

This is an overloaded version of the release() method. Using this, you can actually release the currently held WebElement in the middle of another WebElement. In this way, we don't have to calculate the offset of the target WebElement from the held WebElement.

The API syntax is as follows:

```
public Actions release(WebElement onElement)
```

The input parameter for the preceding method is obviously the target WebElement where the held WebElement should be dropped. The return type is the instance of the Actions class.

Let's modify the preceding code example to use this method:

```
public class ClickAndHoldAndReleaseOnWebElement{
  public static void main(String... args) {
    WebDriver driver = new FirefoxDriver();
    driver.get("file://C:/Sortable.html");
    WebElement three = driver.findElement(By.name("three"));
    WebElement two = driver.findElement(By.name("two"));
    Actions builder = new Actions(driver);
    //Move tile3 to the position of tile2
    builder.clickAndHold(three)
           .release(two)
           .perform();
  }
}
```

Check how simple the preceding code looks. We have removed all the moveByOffset code and added the release() method that takes the WebElement with the name two as the input parameter.

> Invoking the release() or release(WebElement) methods without calling the clickAndHold() method will result in an undefined behavior.

The moveToElement action

The moveToElement() method is another method of WebDriver that helps us to move the mouse cursor to a WebElement on the web page.

The API syntax for the moveToElement() method is as follows:

```
public Actions moveToElement(WebElement toElement)
```

The input parameter for the preceding method is the target WebElement where the mouse should be moved.

Now, go back to *The clickAndHold at current location action* section of this chapter and try to modify the code to use this method. The following is the code we have written in the *The clickAndHold at current location action* section:

```
public class ClickAndHold{
   public static void main(String... args) {
      WebDriver driver = new FirefoxDriver();
      driver.get("file://C:/Sortable.html");
      Actions builder = new Actions(driver);
      //Move tile3 to the position of tile2
      builder.moveByOffset(200, 20)
            .clickAndHold()
            .moveByOffset(120, 0)
            .perform();
   }
}
```

In the preceding code, we will replace the moveByOffset(x, y) method with the moveToElement(WebElement) method:

```
public class ClickAndHold{
   public static void main(String... args) {
      WebDriver driver = new FirefoxDriver();
      driver.get("file://C:/Sortable.html");
      WebElement three = driver.findElement(By.name("three"));
      Actions builder = new Actions(driver);
      //Move tile3 to the position of tile2
      builder.moveToElement(three)
            .clickAndHold()
            .moveByOffset(120, 0)
            .perform();
   }
}
```

In the preceding code, we have moved to tile **3**, clicked and held it, and then moved to the location of tile **2** by specifying its offset. If you want, you can add the release() method before the perform() method.

 There might be a number of ways to achieve the same task. It is up to the user to choose the appropriate ones that best suit the given circumstances.

The dragAndDropBy action

There might be many instances where we may have to drag-and-drop components or WebElements of a web page. We can accomplish that by using many of the actions seen until now. But WebDriver has given us a convenient out of the box method to use. Let's see its API syntax.

The API syntax for the dragAndDropBy() method is as follows:

```
public Actions dragAndDropBy(WebElement source,
int xOffset,int yOffset)
```

The WebElement input parameter is the target WebElement to be dragged, the xOffset parameter is the horizontal offset to be moved, and the yOffset parameter is the vertical offset to be moved.

Let's see a code example for it. Open the HTML file, DragMe.html, provided with this book. You can actually drag that rectangle to any location on the web page. Let's see how we can do that using WebDriver. The following is the code example for that:

```
public class DragMe {
  public static void main(String... args) {
    WebDriver driver = new FirefoxDriver();
    driver.get("file://C:/DragMe.html");
    WebElement dragMe = driver.findElement(By.id("draggable"));
    Actions builder = new Actions(driver);
    builder.dragAndDropBy(dragMe, 300, 200).perform();
  }
}
```

In the preceding code, dragMe is the WebElement that is identified by it's Id, and that is dragged 300px horizontally and 200px vertically.

The dragAndDrop action

The dragAndDrop() method is similar to the dragAndDropBy() method. The only difference being that instead of moving the WebElement by an offset, we move it on to a target element.

The API syntax for the dragAndDrop() method is as follows:

```
public Actions dragAndDrop(WebElement source,
WebElement target)
```

The input parameters for the preceding method are the WebElement source and the WebElement target, while the return type is the Actions class.

Let's see a working code example for it. Open the `DragAndDrop.html` file that is provided with the book. Here we can actually drag the **Drag me to my target** rectangle to the **Drop here** rectangle. Try that. Let's see how that can be achieved using WebDriver:

```
public class DragAndDrop {
  public static void main(String... args) {
    WebDriver driver = new FirefoxDriver();
    driver.get("file://C:/DragAndDrop.html");
    WebElement src = driver.findElement(By.id("draggable"));
    WebElement trgt = driver.findElement(By.id("droppable"));
    Actions builder = new Actions(driver);
    builder.dragAndDrop(src, trgt).perform();
  }
}
```

In the preceding code, the source and target WebElements are identified by their IDs, and the `dragAndDrop()` method is used to drag one to the other.

The doubleClick at current location action

Moving on to another action that can be performed using mouse, `doubleClick()` is another out of the box method that WebDriver provides to emulate the double-clicking of the mouse. This method, like the `click()` method, comes in two flavors. One is double-clicking a WebElement, which we will discuss in next section; the second is clicking at the current location of the cursor, which will be discussed here.

The API syntax is as follows:

```
public Actions doubleClick()
```

Obviously, the preceding method doesn't take any input parameters, as it just clicks on the current cursor location and returns an `Actions` class instance.

Let's see how the previous code can be converted to use this method:

```
public class DoubleClick {
  public static void main(String... args) {
    WebDriver driver = new FirefoxDriver();
    driver.get("file://C:/DoubleClick.html");
    WebElement dblClick= driver.findElement(By.name("dblClick"));
    Actions builder = new Actions(driver);
    builder.moveToElement(dblClick).doubleClick().perform();
  }
}
```

In the preceding code, we have used the `moveToElement(WebElement)` method to move the mouse to the location of the button element, and just double-clicked at the current location.

The doubleClick on WebElement action

Now that we have seen a method that double-clicks at the current location, we will discuss another method that WebDriver provides to emulate the double-clicking of a WebElement.

The API syntax for the `doubleClick()` method is as follows:

```
public Actions doubleClick(WebElement onElement)
```

The input parameter for the preceding method is the target WebElement that has to be double-clicked and the return type is the `Actions` class.

Let's see a code example for this. Now, open the `DoubleClick.html` file, and click (single) on the **Click Me** button. You shouldn't see anything happening. Now double-click on the button; you should see an alert saying **Double Clicked !!**. Now, we try to do the same thing using WebDriver. The following is the code to do that:

```
public class DoubleClick {
    public static void main(String... args) {
        WebDriver driver = new FirefoxDriver();
        driver.get("file://C:/DoubleClick.html");
        WebElement dblClick = driver.findElement(By.name("dblClick"));
        Actions builder = new Actions(driver);
        builder.doubleClick(dblClick).perform();
    }
}
```

After executing the preceding code, you should see an alert dialog saying that the button has been double-clicked.

The contextClick on WebElement action

The `contextClick()` method, also known as right-click, is quite common on many web pages these days. The context is nothing but a menu; a list of items is associated to a WebElement based on the current state of the web page. This context menu can be accessed by a right-click of the mouse on the WebElement. WebDriver provides the developer with an option of emulating that action using the `contextClick()` method. Like many other methods, this method has two variants as well. One is clicking on the current location and the other overloaded method is clicking on the WebElement. Lets discuss the context clicking on WebElement here.

The API syntax for the `contextClick()` method is as follows:

```
public Actions contextClick(WebElement onElement)
```

The input parameter is obviously the WebElement that has to be right-clicked, and the return type is the `Actions` instance.

As we do normally, its time to see a code example. If you open the `ContextClick.html` file, you can right-click on the text visible on the page and it will display the context menu. Now, clicking any item pops up an alert dialog stating which item has been clicked. Now, let's see how to implement this in WebDriver in the following code:

```
public class ContextClick {
  public static void main(String... args) {
    WebDriver driver = new FirefoxDriver();
    driver.get("file://C:/ContextClick.html");
    WebElement contextMenu = driver.findElement(By.id("div-context"));
    Actions builder = new Actions(driver);
    builder.contextClick(contextMenu)
      .click(driver.findElement(By.name("Item 4")))
        .perform();
  }
}
```

In the preceding code, first we have right-clicked using the `contextClick()` method on the WebElement `contextMenu`, and then left-clicked on **Item 4** from the context menu. This should pop up an alert dialog saying **Item 4 Clicked**.

The contextClick at current location action

Now that we have seen context click on a WebElement, its time to explore the `contextClick()` method at the current mouse location.

The API syntax for the `contextClick()` method is as follows:

```
public Actions contextClick()
```

As expected, the preceding method doesn't expect any input parameter, and returns the `Actions` instance. Let's see the necessary modifications needed to the previous example in order to use this method. The following is the code refactored to achieve this:

```
public class ContextClick {
  public static void main(String... args) {
    WebDriver driver = new FirefoxDriver();
```

```
driver.get("file://C:/ContextClick.html");
WebElement contextMenu = driver.findElement(By.id("div-context"));
Actions builder = new Actions(driver);
builder.moveToElement(contextMenu)
        .contextClick()
        .click(driver.findElement(By.name("Item 4")))
        .perform();
    }
}
```

The preceding code first moves the cursor to the `div-context` WebElement, and then context clicks it.

Learning keyboard-based interactions

Until now, we have seen all the actions that can be taken using a mouse. It's time to look at some of the actions that are specific to the keyboard in the `Actions` class. Basically, there are three different actions that are available in the `Actions` class that are specific to the keyboard. They are the `keyUp`, `keyDown`, and `sendKeys` actions, each having two overloaded methods. One method is to execute the action directly on the WebElement, and the other is to just execute the method irrespective of its context.

The keyDown and keyUp actions

The `keyDown()` method is used to simulate the action of pressing and holding a key. The keys that we are referencing here are *Shift*, *Ctrl*, and *Alt* keys. The `keyUp()` method is used to release the key that is already pressed using the `keyDown()` method. The API syntax for the `keyDown()` method is as follows

```
public Actions keyDown(Keys theKey) throws IllegalArgumentException
```

An `IllegalArgumentException` is thrown when the passed key is not one of the *Shift*, *Ctrl*, and *Alt* keys.

The API syntax for the `keyUp()` method is as follows

```
public Actions keyUp(Keys theKey)
```

The `keyUp` action performed on a key, on which a `keyDown` action is not already being performed, will result in some unexpected results. So, we have to make sure we perform the `keyUp` action after a `keyDown` action is performed.

The sendKeys() method

This is used to type in alphanumeric and special character keys into WebElements such as textbox, textarea, and so on. This is different from the `WebElement.sendKeys(CharSequence keysToSend)` method, as this method expects the WebElements to have the focus before being called. The API syntax for the `sendkeys()` method is as follows:

```
public Actions sendKeys(CharSequence keysToSend)
```

We expect you to implement a couple of test scripts around these keyboard events using the `keyUp`, `keyDown`, and `sendKeys()` methods.

Summary

In this chapter, we have learned how to use the `Actions` class to create a set of actions, and build them into a composite action to execute it in one pass using the `perform()` method. In this way, we can aggregate a series of complex user actions into a single functionality, which can be executed in one pass. In the next chapter, we will see some of the features of WebDriver such as capabilities, taking screenshots, and so on.

3

Exploring the Features of WebDriver

Until the previous chapter, we have seen various basic and advanced interactions that a user can perform on a webpage using WebDriver. In this chapter, we will discuss the different capabilities and features of WebDriver that enable the test script developer to have better control on WebDriver and consequently on the web application that is under test. The list of features that we are going to cover in this chapter is as follows:

- Setting the desired capabilities for a browser
- Taking screenshots
- Locating target windows and iFrames
- Exploring Navigate
- Waiting for WebElements to load
- Handling cookies

Let's get started without any further delay.

Setting the desired capabilities for a browser

You, as a user of WebDriver, have the flexibility to create a session for a browser with your own set of desired capabilities that a browser should or shouldn't have. Using the capabilities feature in WebDriver, you are given a way to specify your choice of how your browser should behave.

Some of the examples of browser capabilities include enabling a browser session to support taking screenshots of the webpage, executing custom JavaScript on the webpage, enabling the browser session to interact with window alerts, and so on.

There are many capabilities that are specific to individual browsers, but there are some specific capabilities that are generic to all the browsers. We will discuss some of them here, and the remaining, as and when we come across those features in this book. The browser-specific capabilities will be discussed in greater detail in the next chapter.

Capabilities is an interface in the WebDriver library whose direct implementation is the DesiredCapabilities class. The series of steps involved in creating a browser session with specific capabilities is as follows:

1. Identify all of the capabilities that you want to arm your browser with.

2. Create a DesiredCapabilities class instance and set all of the capabilities to it.

3. Now, create an instance of WebDriver with all of the above capabilities passed to it.

This will create an instance of Firefox/IE/Chrome or whichever browser you have instantiated with all of your desired capabilities.

Let's create an instance of FirefoxDriver while enabling the takesScreenShot capability:

```
public class BrowserCapabilities {
  public static void main(String... args) {
    Map capabilitiesMap = new HashMap();
    capabilitiesMap.put("takesScreenShot", true);
    DesiredCapabilities capabilities
                = new DesiredCapabilities(capabilitiesMap);
    WebDriver driver = new FirefoxDriver(capabilities);
    driver.get("http://www.google.com");
  }
}
```

In the preceding code, we set all of the capabilities that we desire in a map and created an instance of DesiredCapabilities using that map. Now, we have created an instance of FirefoxDriver with these capabilities. This will now launch a Firefox browser that will have support for taking screenshots of the webpage. If you see the definition of the DesiredCapabilities class, the constructor of the class is overloaded in many different ways. Passing a map is one of them. You can use the default constructor and create an instance of the DesiredCapabilities class, and then set the capabilities using the setCapability() method.

Some of the default capabilities that are common across browsers are shown in the following table:

Capability	What it is used for
takesScreenShot	Tells whether the browser session can take a screenshot of the webpage
handlesAlert	Tells whether the browser session can handle modal dialogs
cssSelectorsEnabled	Tells whether the browser session can use CSS selectors while searching for elements
javascriptEnabled	Enables/disables user-supplied JavaScript execution in the context of the webpage
acceptSSLCerts	Enables/disables the browser to accept all of the SSL certificates by default
webStorageEnabled	This is an HTML5 feature, and it is possible to enable or disable the browser session to interact with storage objects

There are many other capabilities of WebDriver, and we will talk about them when we cover individual features; some in this chapter, and the remaining in the upcoming chapters.

Taking screenshots

Taking a screenshot of a webpage is a very useful capability of WebDriver. This is very handy when your test case fails, and you want to see the state of the application when the test case failed. The TakesScreenShot interface in the WebDriver library is implemented by all of the different variants of WebDriver, such as Firefox Driver, Internet Explorer Driver, Chrome Driver, and so on.

The TakesScreenShot capability is enabled in all of the browsers by default. Because this is a read-only capability, a user doesn't have much say on toggling it. Before we see a code example that uses this capability, we should look at an important method of the TakesScreenShot interface—getScreenshotAs().

The API syntax for getScreenshotAs() is as follows:

```
public <X> X getScreenshotAs(OutputType<X> target)
```

Here, OutputType is another interface of the WebDriver lib. We can ask WebDriver to give your screenshot in three different formats; they are: BASE64, BYTES (raw data), and FILE. If you choose the FILE format, it writes the data into a .png file, which will be deleted once the JVM is killed. So, you should always copy that file into a safe location so that it can be used for later reference.

The return type is a specific output that depends on the selected OutputType. For example, selecting OutputType.BYTES will return a byte array, and selecting OutputType.FILE will return a file object.

Depending on the browser used, the output screenshot will be one of the following in the order of preference:

- The entire page

- The current window

- A visible portion of the current frame

- The screenshot of the entire display containing the browser

- For example, if you are using Firefox Driver, getScreenshotAs() takes the screenshot of the entire page, but Chrome Driver returns only the visible portion of the current frame.

- It's time to take a look at the following code example:

```
public class TakesScreenShotExample{
   public static void main(String... args) {
      WebDriver driver = new FirefoxDriver();
      driver.get("http://www.packtpub.com/");
      File scrFile = ((TakesScreenShot)driver).
getScreenshotAs(OutputType.FILE);
      System.out.println(scrFile.getAbsolutePath());
   }
}
```

- In the preceding code, we have used the getScreenshotAs() method to take the screenshot of the webpage and save it to a file format. The getAbsolutePath() method returns the path of the saved image, which you can open and examine.

 The file to which the screenshot data is written is a temporary file and will be deleted as soon as the JVM exits. So it is a good idea to copy the file before the test completes.

Locating target windows and iFrames

WebDriver enables the developers to switch easily between the multiple windows or frames an application loads in. For instance, when you click on the Internet banking link on a bank web application, it will open the Internet banking application in a separate window. At this point, you may want to switch back to the original window to handle some events. Similarly, you may have to deal with a web application that is divided into two frames on the web page. The frame on the left may contain navigation items, and the frame on the right displays the appropriate web page based on what is selected in the frame on the left. Using WebDriver, you can develop test cases that can easily handle such complex situations.

The `WebDriver.TargetLocator` interface is used to locate a given frame or window. In this section, we will see how WebDriver handles switching between browser windows and between two frames in the same window.

Switching among windows

First, we will see a code example for handling multiple windows. For this chapter, there is an HTML file provided with this book named `Window.html`. It is a very basic web page that links to the Google Search page. When you click on the link, the Google Search page is opened in a different window. Every time you open a web page using WebDriver in a browser window, WebDriver assigns a window handle to that. WebDriver uses this identifier to identify the window. At this point, in your WebDriver, there are two window handles registered. Now, on the screen, you can see that the Google Search page is in the front and has the focus. At this point, if you want to switch to the first browser window, you can use WebDriver's `switchTo()` method to do that.

The API syntax for `TargetLocator` is as follows:

```
WebDriver.TargetLocator switchTo()
```

This method returns the `WebDriver.TargetLocator` instance, where you can tell the WebDriver whether to switch between browser windows or frames. Let's see how WebDriver deals with this:

```
public class WindowHandling {
    public static void main(String... args){
        WebDriver driver = new FirefoxDriver();
        driver.get("file://C:/Window.html");

        String window1 = driver.getWindowHandle();
        System.out.println("First Window Handle is: "+window1);
```

```
        WebElement link = driver.findElement(By.linkText("Google
Search"));
        link.click();

        String window2 = driver.getWindowHandle();
        System.out.println("Second Window Handle is: "+window2);
        System.out.println("Number of Window Handles so for: "
                +driver.getWindowHandles().size());

        driver.switchTo().window(window1);

    }
}
```

Observe the following line in the preceding code:

```
        String window1 = driver.getWindowHandle();
```

Here, the driver returns the assigned identifier for the window. Now, before we move on to a different window, it is better to store this value so that if we want to switch back to this window, we can use this handle or identifier. In order to retrieve all of the window handles that are registered with your driver so far, you can use the following method:

```
        driver.getWindowHandles()
```

This will return the set of identifiers of all of the browser window handles opened in the driver session so far. Now, in our example, after we open the Google Search page, the window corresponding to it is shown in front with the focus. If you want to go back to the first window, we have to use the following code:

```
        driver.switchTo().window(window1);
```

This will bring the first window into focus.

Switching among frames

Let us now see how we can handle switching among the frames of a web page. In the HTML files supplied with this book, you will see a file named Frames.html. If you open that, you will see two HTML files loaded in two different frames. Let Let's see how we can switch between them and type into the text boxes available in each frame.

```
    public class SwitchBetweenFrames {
        public static void main(String... args) {
            WebDriver driver = new FirefoxDriver();
            driver.get("file://C:/Frames.html");
```

```
        Actions action = new Actions(driver);

        driver.switchTo().frame(0);
        WebElement txt = driver.findElement(By.name("1"));
        txt.sendKeys("I'm Frame One");

        driver.switchTo().defaultContent();

        driver.switchTo().frame(1);
        txt = driver.findElement(By.name("2"));
        txt.sendKeys("I'm Frame Two");
    }
}
```

In the preceding code, we have used `switchTo().frame` instead of `switchTo().window` because we are moving across frames.

The API syntax for frame is as follows:

```
WebDriver frame(int index)
```

This method takes the index of the frame that you want to switch to. If your web page has three frames, WebDriver indexes them as 0, 1, and 2 where the zero index is assigned to the first frame encountered in the DOM. Similarly, you can switch among frames using their names by using the overloaded method of the above. The API syntax is as follows:.

```
WebDriver frame(String frameNameOrframeID)
```

You can pass the name of the frame or its ID. Using this, you can switch to the frame if you are not sure about the index of the target frame. The other overloaded method is as follows:

```
WebDriver frame(WebElement frameElement)
```

The input parameter is the `WebElement` of the frame.

Coming back to our code example; first, we have switched to our first frame and typed into the text field. Then, instead of directly switching to the second frame, we have come to the main or default content, and then switched to the second frame. The code for that is as follows:

```
driver.switchTo().defaultContent();
```

This is very important. If you don't do this, and try to switch to the second frame while you are still in the first frame, your WebDriver will complain, saying that it couldn't find a frame with index 1. This is because the WebDriver searches for the second frame in the context of the first frame, which is obviously not available. So, you have to first come to the top-level container and switch to the frame you are interested in.

After switching to the default content, you can now switch to the second frame using the following code:

```
driver.switchTo().frame(1);
```

Thus, you can switch between the frames and execute the corresponding WebDriver actions.

Handling alerts

Apart from switching between windows and frames, you may have to handle various modal dialogs in a web application. For this, WebDriver provides an API to handle alert dialogs. The API for that is as follows:

```
Alert alert()
```

The preceding method will switch to the currently active modal dialog on the web page. This returns an `Alert` instance where appropriate actions can be taken on that dialog. If there is no dialog currently present, and you invoke this API, it throws back a `NoAlertPresentException`.

The `Alert` interface contains a number of APIs to execute different actions. The following list discusses them one after the other:

- `void accept()`: This is equivalent to the **OK** button action on the dialog. The corresponding **OK** button actions are invoked when the `accept()` action is taken on a dialog.
- `void dismiss()`: This is equivalent to clicking on the **CANCEL** action button.
- `java.lang.String getText()`: This will return the text that appears on the dialog. This can be used if you want to evaluate the text on the modal dialog.
- `void sendKeys(java.lang.String keysToSend)`: This will allow the developer to type in some text into the alert if the alert has some provision for it.

Exploring Navigate

As we know, WebDriver talks to individual browsers natively. This way it has better control, not just on the web page, but on the browser itself. **Navigate** is one such feature of WebDriver that allows the test script developer to work with the browser's Back, Forward, and Refresh controls. As users of a web page, quite often, we use the browser's Back and Forward controls to navigate between the pages of a single application, or sometimes, multiple applications. As a test script developer, you may want to develop tests that observe the behavior of the application when browser navigation buttons are clicked, especially the Back button. For example, if you use your navigation button in a banking application, the session should expire and the user should be logged out. So, using the WebDriver's navigation feature, you can emulate those actions.

The method that is used for this purpose is navigate(). The following is its API syntax:

```
WebDriver.Navigation navigate()
```

Obviously, there is no input parameter for this method, but the return type is the WebDriver.Navigation interface, which contains all of the browser navigation options that help you navigate through your browser's history.

Now let's see a code example and then analyze the code:

```
public class WebDriverNavigate{
  public static void main(String... args) {
    WebDriver driver = new FirefoxDriver();
    driver.navigate().to("http://www.google.com");

    WebElement searchBox = driver.findElement(By.name("q"));
    searchBox.sendKeys("Selenium WebDriver");
    WebElement searchButton = driver.findElement(By.name("btnG"));
    searchButton.click();
    searchBox.clear();
    searchBox.sendKeys("Packt Publishing");
    searchButton.click();

    driver.navigate().back();
    driver.navigate().forward();
    driver.navigate().refresh();
  }
}
```

The preceding code opens the Google Search page, and at first, searches for the text `Selenium WebDriver`; then, after the search results are loaded, it does a second search for `Packt Publishing` and waits for the results. Now that we have a navigation history created in the browser, it uses WebDriver navigation to go back in the browser history, then go forward and refresh the page.

Let's analyze the navigation methods used in the preceding code. The line of code that initially loads the Google web page uses the `to()` method of the `Navigation` class as follows:

```
driver.navigate().to("http://www.google.com");
```

Here, first `driver.navigate()` returns the `WebDriver.Navigation` interface on which the `to()` method is used to navigate to a web URL. The API syntax is as follows:

```
void to(java.lang.String url)
```

The input parameter for this method is the `url` string that has to be loaded in the browser. This method will load the page in the browser by using the `HTTP GET` operation, and it will block everything else until the page is completely loaded. This method is the same as the `driver.get(String url)` method.

The `WebDriver.Navigation` interface also provides an overloaded method of this `to()` method to make it easy to pass the URL. The API syntax for it is as follows:

```
void to(java.net.URL url)
```

Next, in the code example, we did a couple of searches for `Selenium WebDriver` and `Packt Publishing`. Then, we tried to use Navigation's `back()` method to emulate our browser's Back button using the following line of code:

```
driver.navigate().back();
```

This will take the browser to the Selenium WebDriver search results page. The API syntax for this method is pretty straightforward, as follows:

```
void back()
```

This method doesn't take any input and doesn't return anything as well, but takes the browser one level back in its history.

Then, the next method in the navigation is the `forward()` method, which is pretty much similar to the `back()` method, but takes the browser one level in the opposite direction. In the preceding code example, invoking the following should take the browser to the `Packt Publishing` search results:

```
driver.navigate().forward();
```

The API syntax for the method is as follows:

```
void forward()
```

This method doesn't take any input and doesn't return anything as well, but takes the browser one level forward in its history.

The last line of code in the code example uses the refresh() method of WebDriver's navigation:

```
driver.navigate().refresh();
```

This method will reload the current URL to emulate the browser's refresh (*F5* key) action. The API syntax is as follows:

```
void refresh()
```

As you can see, the syntax is very similar to the back() and forward() methods, and this method will reload the current URL. Hence, these are the various methods WebDriver provides the developers to emulate some browser actions.

Waiting for WebElements to load

If you have a previous WebUI automation experience, I'm sure you would have come across a situation where your test script couldn't find an element on the webpage as the webpage is still loading. This could happen due to various reasons. One classic example is when the application server or webserver is serving the page too slowly due to resource constraints; the other could be when you are accessing the page on a very slow network. The reason could be that the element on the webpage is not loaded by the time your test script tries to find it. This is where you have to calculate and configure the average wait time your test scripts should wait for WebElements to load on the webpage.

WebDriver provides the test script developers a very handy feature to manage wait time. **Wait time** is the time your driver will wait for the WebElement to load before it gives up and throws NoSuchElementException. Remember, in *Chapter 1, Introducing WebDriver and WebElements*, we have discussed the findElement(By by) method that throws NoSuchElementException when it cannot find the target WebElement.

There are two ways by which you can make WebDriver wait for WebElement. They are **implicit wait time** and **Explicit wait time**. Implicit timeouts are common to all the WebElements and has a global timeout period associated to it, but the explicit timeouts can be configured to individual WebElements. Let's discuss each of them here.

Implicit wait time

Implicit wait time is used when you want to configure the WebDriver's wait time as a whole for the application under test. Imagine you have hosted a web application on a local server and on a remote server. Obviously, the time to load for a webpage hosted on a local server would be less than the time for the same page hosted on a remote server, due to network latency. Now, if you want to execute your test cases against each of them, you may have to configure the wait time accordingly, such that your test case doesn't end up spending more time waiting for the page or spend far too less time and timeout. To handle these kind of wait time issues, WebDriver gives an option to set the implicit wait time for all of the operations that the driver does using the `manage()` method.

Let's see a code example of implicit wait time:

```
public class ImplicitWaitTime {

    public static void main(String... args) {
        WebDriver driver = new FirefoxDriver();
        driver.manage().timeouts().implicitlyWait(10,    TimeUnit.
SECONDS);
        driver.get("www.google.com");
    }
}
```

Let us analyze the following highlighted line of code:

```
driver.manage().timeouts().implicitlyWait(10,    TimeUnit.SECONDS);
```

Here, `driver.manage().timeouts()` returns `WebDriver.Timeouts` interface, which declares a method named `implicitlyWait`, which is where you specify the amount of time the driver should wait when searching for a WebElement on a webpage if it is not immediately present. Periodically, the WebDriver will poll for the WebElement on the webpage until the maximum wait time specified to the previous method is over. In the preceding code, 10 seconds is the maximum wait time your driver will wait for any WebElement to load on your browser. If it loads within this time period, WebDriver proceeds with the rest of the code; else, it will throw a `NoSuchElementException`.

Use this method when you want to specify a maximum wait time, which is generally common for most of the WebElements on your web application. The various factors that influence the performance of your page are network bandwidth, server configuration, and so on. Based on those conditions, as a developer of your WebDriver test cases, you have to arrive at a value for the maximum implicit wait time, such that your test cases don't take too long to execute and at the same time don't timeout very frequently.

Explicit wait time

Implicit timeout is generic to all the WebElements of a web page. But, if you have one specific WebElement in your application where you want to wait for a very long time, this approach may not work. Setting the implicit wait time to the value of this very long time period will delay your entire test suite execution. So you have to make an exception for only a particular case, like this WebElement. To handle such scenarios, WebDriver has explicit wait time for a WebElement.

So let's see how you can wait for a particular WebElement using WebDriver with the following code:

```
public class ExplicitWaitTime {
    public static void main(String... args) {
        WebDriver driver = new FirefoxDriver();
        driver.get("http://www.google.com");
        WebElement element = (new WebDriverWait(driver, 20)).until(new
ExpectedCondition<WebElement>() {
            @Override
            public WebElement apply(WebDriver d) {
                return d.findElement(By.name("q"));
            }
        });
    }
}
```

The highlighted code is where we have created a conditional wait for a particular WebElement. The ExpectedCondition interface can be used to apply the conditional wait on a WebElement. Here, WebDriver will wait for a maximum of 20 seconds for this particular WebElement. The implicit timeout doesn't get applied for this WebElement. If the WebElement doesn't load within the 20 seconds maximum wait time, as we know, the driver throws a NoSuchElementException. Thus, you can override the implicit wait time exclusively for the WebElements you think will take more time by using this handy explicit wait time.

Handling cookies

Let's say you are automating the Facebook webpage. There could be many scenarios you want to automate, such as writing on your wall, writing on your friend's wall, reading other walls, adding friends, deleting friends, and so on. For all these actions, one common thing is to have to log in to Facebook in each of the test cases. So, logging in to Facebook in every test case of yours will increase the overall test execution time significantly. To reduce the execution time of your test cases, you can actually skip signing in for every test case. This can be done by signing in for one time and writing all the cookies of that domain into a file. From the next login onwards, you can actually load the cookies from the file and add to the driver.

To fetch all of the cookies that are loaded for a webpage, WebDriver provides the following method:

```
driver.manage().getCookies()
```

This will return all of the cookies that the web page stores in the current session. Each cookie is associated with a name, value, domain, path, expiry, and the status of whether it is secure or not. The server to validate a client cookie parses all of these values. Now, we will store all of this information for each cookie in a file so that our individual test cases read from this file and load that information into the driver. Hence, you can skip the login, because once your driver session has this information in it, the Facebook server treats your browser session as authenticated and directly takes you to your requested URL.

The following is a quick code to store the cookie information:

```
package com.packt.webdriver.chapter3;

import java.io.BufferedWriter;
import java.io.File;
import java.io.FileWriter;

import org.openqa.selenium.By;
import org.openqa.selenium.Cookie;
import org.openqa.selenium.WebDriver;
import org.openqa.selenium.firefox.FirefoxDriver;

public class StoreCookieInfo {

  public static void main(String... args) {
    WebDriver driver = new FirefoxDriver();
    driver.get("http://www.facebook.com");
    driver.findElement(By.name("email")).sendKeys("<<ur mailID>>");
    driver.findElement(By.name("pass")).sendKeys("<<ur password>>");
    driver.findElement(By.name("persistent")).click();
    driver.findElement(By.name("pass")).submit();

    File f = new File("browser.data");
    try{
        f.delete();
        f.createNewFile();
        FileWriter fos = new FileWriter(f);
        BufferedWriter bos = new BufferedWriter(fos);
```

```
            for(Cookie ck : driver.manage().getCookies()) {
                    bos.write((ck.getName()+";"+ck.getValue()+";"+ck.
getDomain()
                        +";"+ck.getPath()+";"+ck.getExpiry()+";"+ck.
isSecure())));
                bos.newLine();
            }
            bos.flush();
            bos.close();
            fos.close();
        }catch(Exception ex){
            ex.printStackTrace();
        }


    }
}
```

From now on, for every test case or a set of test cases, load the cookie information from the browser.data file, and add it to the driver using the following method:

```
driver.manage().addCookie(ck);
```

After you add this information to your browser session and go to the Facebook page, it will automatically redirect you to the home page without asking for a login, thus avoiding a login every time for every test case. The code that adds all of the previous cookies to the driver is as follows:

```
package com.packt.webdriver.chapter3;

import java.io.BufferedReader;
import java.io.File;
import java.io.FileReader;
import java.util.Date;
import java.util.StringTokenizer;

import org.openqa.selenium.Cookie;
import org.openqa.selenium.WebDriver;
import org.openqa.selenium.firefox.FirefoxDriver;

public class LoadCookieInfo {

    public static void main(String... args){
        WebDriver driver = new FirefoxDriver();
        driver.get("http://www.facebook.com");
        try{
```

```
            File f = new File("browser.data");
            FileReader fr = new FileReader(f2);
            BufferedReader br = new BufferedReader(fr);
            String line;
            while((line=br.readLine())!=null){
                StringTokenizer str = new StringTokenizer(line,";");
                while(str.hasMoreTokens()){
                    String name = str.nextToken();
                    String value = str.nextToken();
                    String domain = str.nextToken();
                    String path = str.nextToken();
                    Date expiry = null;
                    String dt;
                    if(!(dt=str.nextToken()).equals("null")){
                        expiry = new Date(dt);
                    }
                    boolean isSecure = new Boolean(str.nextToken()).
booleanValue();
                    Cookie ck = new Cookie(name,value,domain,path,expi
ry,isSecure);
                    driver.manage().addCookie(ck);
                }
            }
        }catch(Exception ex){
            ex.printStackTrace();
        }
        driver.get("http://www.facebook.com");
    }
}
```

Thus, we can be directly taken to the home page without logging in again and again. If you observe, after creating the driver instance, we have the following line:

```
driver.get("http://www.facebook.com");
```

Ideally, this line should be visible after we have set the cookies to the driver. But the reason it is at the top is because the WebDriver doesn't allow you to set the cookies directly into this session, because it treats those cookies as if they are from a different domain. Try removing the previous line of code and execute it, and you will see the error. So, initially you will try to visit the Facebook page to set the domain value of the driver to Facebook and load all of the cookies. When you execute this code, initially you will see the login page of Facebook, and you will be automatically taken to the home page when the same code at the end is invoked again after the cookies are loaded.

Thus, you can avoid entering the username and password on the server validating them again and again for each test, and thereby save a lot of time by using the WebDriver's cookies feature.

Summary

In this chapter, we have discussed the various features of WebDriver. Using these features will help you test your target web application more effectively by designing more innovating test frameworks and test cases.

In the next chapter, we will look at the different available WebDriver implementations.

4
Different Available WebDrivers

All this while in the previous chapters, we have discussed many features of WebDriver using FirefoxDriver. Similar to FirefoxDriver, which is an implementation of WebDriver specific to the Firefox browser, we have many other implementations of WebDriver specific to various other browsers, such as Internet Explorer, Chrome, Safari, and Opera. In this chapter, we will go through details of each of these implementations starting with Firefox Driver. Though all these implementations have all the features of WebDriver that we have discussed so far, there are a few things that are specific to a particular browser implementation. In the chapter, we will concentrate more on these specifics.

FirefoxDriver

The FirefoxDriver works as an extension to the Firefox browser. It uses the **XPCOM (Cross Platform Component Object Model)** framework of Mozilla to execute the commands sent by the language bindings. Language bindings communicate with the extension, that is, FirefoxDriver, by connecting over a socket and sending commands. This socket is bound to a port, which is called the locking port; typically, it would be 7055. The reason it is called the locking port is because it is used as a mutex so that it allows only one instance of Firefox to listen to a Firefox Driver on that port.

After this socket is established, the client language binding (in our case, the Java binding) sends the commands to the Firefox extension in a serialized JSON format. The JSON format contains the following components:

- **Context**: This is the current window or frame
- **CommandName**: For example, DragAndDrop, SendKeys

- **Parameters**: This can be empty, or sometimes the text will need to be typed
- **ElementId**: This is the ID of the element on which the action has to be performed

This serialized JSON is sent over the socket or wire established earlier to the Firefox Extension or FirefoxDriver. This is the reason Selenium-2 or WebDriver is said to be working on `JSON-Wire` protocol.

Once the commands reach from the client language bindings to the FirefoxDriver, it deserializes the JSON, and the commands are interpreted and looked up in the Firefox Driver prototype, which are the JavaScript functions for each command. After execution, the response is sent back via the socket to the client. This response is again a JSON that contains `methodName` (this is same as the `commandName` in the request), `Context`, `isError` (indicating if an error has occurred, so that the client can thrown an exception), and `ResponseText` (the output of the command executed).

Now that we have seen the basic flow of how the Firefox Driver works, in the following section, we will learn about the Firefox browser, how it maintains user profiles, its preferences, and how you can deal with them using Firefox WebDriver. As you know, different browsers have different ways and mechanisms to deal with its user's choices and preferences. Similarly, Firefox has its own way. To start with, let us take a look at what a Firefox profile is.

Understanding the Firefox profile

A Firefox profile is a folder that the Firefox browser uses to store all your passwords, bookmarks, settings, and all other user data. A Firefox user can create any number of profiles with different custom settings and use it accordingly. According to Mozilla, the following are the different attributes that can be stored in the profiles:

- Bookmarks and browsing history
- Passwords
- Site-specific preferences
- Search engines
- A personal dictionary
- Autocomplete history
- Download history
- Cookies
- DOM Storage
- Security certificate settings

- Security device settings

- Download actions

- Plugin MIME types

- Stored sessions

- Toolbar customizations

- User styles

To create, rename, or delete a profile, you have to perform the following steps:

1. Open the Firefox profile manager. To do that, in the command prompt terminal, you have to navigate to the install directory of Firefox; typically, it would in **Program Files** if you are on Windows. Navigate to the location where you can find the `firefox.exe` file, and execute the following command:

   ```
   firefox.exe -p
   ```

   It will open the profile manager that will look like the following screenshot:

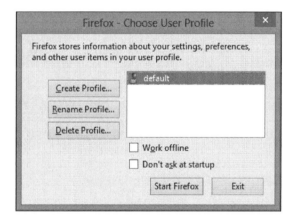

   Note that before executing the above command, you need to make sure you close all your currently running Firefox instances.

2. Use the **Create Profile...** button to create another profile, **Rename Profile...** button to rename an existing profile, and **Delete Profile...** button to delete one.

So, coming back to our WebDriver, whenever we create an instance of FirefoxDriver, a temporary profile is created and used by the WebDriver. To see the profile that is currently being used by a Firefox instance, you have to navigate to **Help | Troubleshooting Information**.

This will launch all the details of that particular Firefox instance of which the profile is a part. It will look similar to the following screenshot:

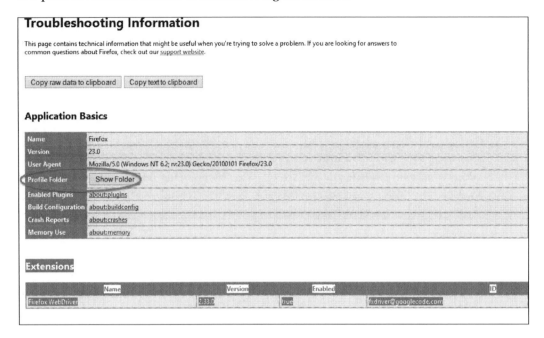

The highlighted oval in the preceding screenshot shows the profile folder. Click on the **Show Folder** button; it should open the location of the profile corresponding to that of your current Firefox instance. Now, let's launch a Firefox browser instance using our FirefoxDriver, and verify its profile location.

Let's launch a Firefox browser using the following code:

```
public class FirefoxProfile {

  public static void main(String... args) {
    FirefoxDriver driver = new FirefoxDriver();
    driver.get("http://www.google.com");
  }

}
```

This will launch a browser instance. Now navigate to **Help | Troubleshooting Information**, and once the info is launched, click the **Show Folder** button. This will open the current WebDriver's profile directory. Every time you launch a Firefox instance using Firefox Driver, it will create a new profile for you. If you go one level above this directory, you will see the profiles created by your FirefoxDriver, as shown in the following screenshot:

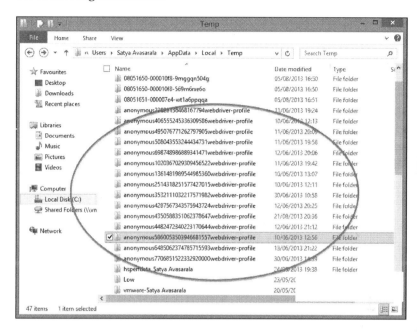

All the above folders correspond to each of the Firefox instances launched by the FirefoxDriver.

Until now, we have seen what Firefox profiles are and how WebDriver creates one every time it launches the browser. Now, let's see how we can create our own custom profiles using WebDriver APIs. The following is the code example to create your own Firefox profile using the WebDriver library and set in it the options you want your browser to have, overriding what FirefoxDriver gives you:

```
public class FirefoxCustomProfile {

    public static void main(String... args){
        FirefoxProfile profile = new FirefoxProfile();

        FirefoxDriver driver = new FirefoxDriver(profile);
        driver.get("http://www.google.com");
    }
}
```

In the preceding code, `FirefoxCustomProfile` is the class that has been instantiated to create our custom profile for our Firefox browser. Now, having an instance of that class, we can set various options and preferences in it, which we will discuss shortly. Before we go to that, there are two overloaded versions of constructors for FirefoxProfile. One creates an empty profile and molds it according to requirements. This is seen in the preceding code. The second version creates a profile instance from an existing profile directory as follows:

```
public FirefoxProfile(java.io.File profileDir)
```

Here, the input parameter `profileDir` is the directory location of any existing profile. The profile directory is the one that we saw in the preceding screenshot.

Let us discuss some interesting customizations or tailoring that we can do to our Firefox browser using Firefox profiles.

Adding the extension to Firefox

In this section, we will see how we can extend our Firefox test browser with some additional capabilities. As we are familiar with our Firebug extension, we will try to extend our test Firefox browser to have this extension. If you observe, though we have installed the Firebug extension to our Firefox, when the tests execute using our FirefoxDriver, we don't see the Firebug extension to the test browser. This is because the profiles that are being used are different. Whenever WebDriver launches a new Firefox browser, it creates a new profile on the disk, and this profile doesn't contain the Firebug extension in it. The following is the screenshot of the Firefox browser that you launch as a user:

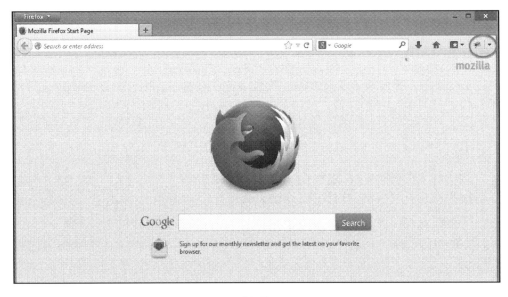

The Firebug plugin is visible on the top-right part of the browser. Now, if you launch the browser using WebDriver, you will not see the plugin attached to it. The following is the screenshot showing that:

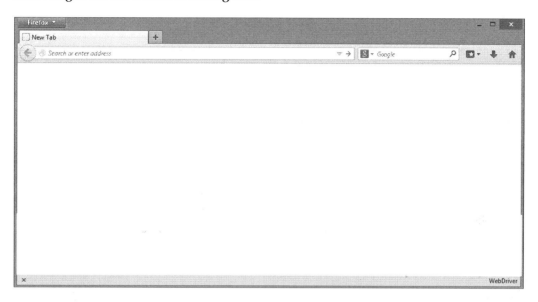

As you can see, the browser where you have installed Firebug as an extension shows it, but the Firefox launched by WebDriver doesn't have that extension. After all, that's WebDriver's default profile. Now, let's change its profile using the addExtension() method provided by FirefoxProfile. This method is used to add extensions to the Firefox browser. The following is the API syntax for the method:

```
public void addExtension(java.io.File extensionToInstall)
   throws java.io.IOException
```

The input parameter is the XPI file that has to be installed on the Firefox browser. If WebDriver doesn't find the file in the specified location, it will raise an IOException.

The following is the code to override the default profile and extend the Firefox browser to have the Firebug extension. Along with the book is the Firebug extension provided. Point to that in your code when you execute it as follows:

```
public class AddExtensionToProfile {
  public static void main(String... args){
    FirefoxProfile profile = new FirefoxProfile();

    try {
      profile.addExtension(new File("C:\\firebug-1.12.0-fx.xpi"));
    } catch (IOException e) {
      e.printStackTrace();
```

```
        }
        FirefoxDriver driver = new FirefoxDriver(profile);
    }
}
```

Now, if you see the Firefox browser that is launched by the FirefoxDriver, you will find the Firebug extension installed on it, as shown in the following screenshot:

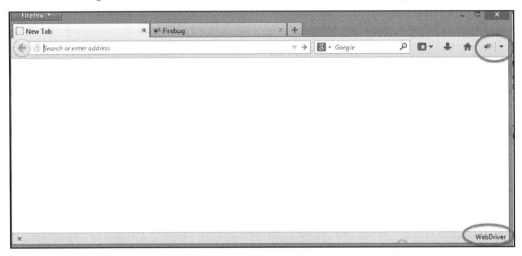

Storing and retrieving a profile

We can also write the profile information of the browser to the JSON file and can later instantiate new browsers with the same profile. The FirefoxProfile class does provide a method to export the profile information as JSON. The following is its API syntax:

```
public String toJson()
```

The output or return type is a String, which contains the JSON information in it.

Now, to create a browser with the same profile, the FirefoxProfile class provides a static method that takes the JSON string as the input. The following is the API syntax:

```
public static FirefoxProfile fromJson(java.lang.String json)throws
    java.io.IOException
```

This is a static method in the FirefoxProfile class that takes the JSON string to create a profile from. The following is the code example for that:

```
public class StoringAndCreatingTheProfile {
    public static void main(String... args){
```

```
FirefoxProfile profile = new FirefoxProfile();
String json="";
try {
  profile.addExtension(new File("C:\\firebug-1.12.0-fx.xpi"));
  json = profile.toJson();
  System.out.println(json);
} catch (IOException e) {
  e.printStackTrace();
}


try {
  FirefoxDriver driver = new
    FirefoxDriver(FirefoxProfile.fromJson(json));
} catch (IOException e) {
  e.printStackTrace();
}


}

}
```

In the preceding code, in the first `try-catch` block, we have exported the profile as a JSON string. In your test case, you can write that JSON information to a file and store it. Later, you can read the JSON file and create a FirefoxDriver from that, as we did in the second `try-catch` block.

Dealing with Firefox preferences

Until now, we have seen how Firefox profiles are, and how we can create our own customized profiles for Firefox Driver. Now, let us see how we can set our preferences in the profiles we create and where FirefoxDriver stores them.

According to Mozilla, a Firefox Preference is any value or defined behavior that can be set by a user. These values are saved to the preference files. If you open the profile directory by navigating to **Help | Troubleshooting Information** and clicking on the **Show Folder** button, you will see two preference files; they are prefs.js and user.js. All the user preferences are written to the prefs.js file by the Firefox application during the launch. A user can override those values to those of his/her choice, and they are stored in the user.js file. The value in user.js for a preference takes precedence over all the other values set for that particular preference. So, your FirefoxDriver overwrites all the default preferences of Firefox in the user.js file for you. When you add a new preference, FirefoxDriver writes that to the user.js preference file, and the Firefox browser behaves accordingly.

Now, let us see the default preferences that FirefoxDriver writes to the `user.js` file:

```
public class SettingPreferences {

  public static void main(String... args){
    FirefoxProfile profile = new FirefoxProfile();

    FirefoxDriver driver = new FirefoxDriver(profile);
    driver.get("http://www.google.com");

  }
}
```

In the preceding code, we are not setting any preferences, but it will still launch the Firefox browser. Now, open the `user.js` file in the profile directory. The following are the list of all the preferences that FirefoxDriver sets for you by default:

```
user_pref("extensions.update.notifyUser", false);
user_pref("security.warn_entering_secure.show_once", false);
user_pref("devtools.errorconsole.enabled", true);
user_pref("extensions.update.enabled", false);
user_pref("browser.dom.window.dump.enabled", true);
user_pref("offline-apps.allow_by_default", true);
user_pref("dom.disable_open_during_load", false);
user_pref("extensions.blocklist.enabled", false);
user_pref("browser.startup.page", 0);
user_pref("toolkit.telemetry.rejected", true);
user_pref("prompts.tab_modal.enabled", false);
user_pref("app.update.enabled", false);
user_pref("app.update.auto", false);
user_pref("toolkit.networkmanager.disable", true);
user_pref("browser.startup.homepage", "about:blank");
user_pref("network.manage-offline-status", false);
user_pref("browser.search.update", false);
user_pref("toolkit.telemetry.enabled", false);
user_pref("browser.link.open_newwindow", 2);
user_pref("browser.EULA.override", true);
user_pref("extensions.autoDisableScopes", 10);
user_pref("browser.EULA.3.accepted", true);
user_pref("security.warn_entering_weak", false);
user_pref("toolkit.telemetry.prompted", 2);
user_pref("browser.safebrowsing.enabled", false);
user_pref("security.warn_entering_secure", false);
user_pref("security.warn_leaving_secure.show_once", false);
user_pref("webdriver_accept_untrusted_certs", true);
user_pref("browser.download.manager.showWhenStarting", false);
user_pref("dom.max_script_run_time", 30);
```

```
user_pref("javascript.options.showInConsole", true);
user_pref("network.http.max-connections-per-server", 10);
user_pref("network.http.phishy-userpass-length", 255);
user_pref("extensions.logging.enabled", true);
user_pref("security.warn_leaving_secure", false);
user_pref("browser.offline", false);
user_pref("browser.link.open_external", 2);
user_pref("signon.rememberSignons", false);
user_pref("webdriver_enable_native_events", true);
user_pref("browser.tabs.warnOnClose", false);
user_pref("security.fileuri.origin_policy", 3);
user_pref("security.fileuri.strict_origin_policy", false);
user_pref("webdriver_assume_untrusted_issuer", true);
user_pref("startup.homepage_welcome_url", "");
user_pref("browser.shell.checkDefaultBrowser", false);
user_pref("browser.safebrowsing.malware.enabled", false);
user_pref("security.warn_submit_insecure", false);
user_pref("webdriver_firefox_port", 7055);
user_pref("dom.report_all_js_exceptions", true);
user_pref("security.warn_viewing_mixed", false);
user_pref("browser.sessionstore.resume_from_crash", false);
user_pref("browser.tabs.warnOnOpen", false);
user_pref("security.warn_viewing_mixed.show_once", false);
user_pref("security.warn_entering_weak.show_once", false);
```

This Firefox Driver treats them as `Frozen Preferences` and doesn't allow the test script developer to change them. However, there are a few preferences in the preceding list that FirefoxDriver allows you to change, which we will see shortly.

Setting preferences

Now we will learn how to set our own preferences. As an example, we will see how to change the user agent of your browser. Many web applications these days are have the main/normal site as well as the mobile site / `m.` site. The application will validate the user agent of the incoming request and accordingly decide whether to act as a server for a normal site or mobile site. So, in order to test your mobile site from your laptop or desktop browser, you just have to change your user agent. Let us see a code example where we can change the user agent preference of our Firefox browser using FirefoxDriver, and send a request to the Google Search page. But before going to that, let's see the `setPreference()` method provided by the `FirefoxProfile` class:

```
public void setPreference(java.lang.String key,
    String value)
```

The input parameters are: key, which is a string and represents your preference; and value, which has to be set to the preference.

There are two other overloaded versions of the preceding method shown; one of which is as follows:

```
public void setPreference(java.lang.String key,
    int value)
```

The other overloaded version is as follows:

```
public void setPreference(java.lang.String key,boolean value)
```

Now, using the preceding setPreference() method, we will try to change the user agent of our browser using the following code:

```
public class SettingPreferences {

    public static void main(String... args){
        FirefoxProfile profile = new FirefoxProfile();

        profile.setPreference("general.useragent.override", "Mozilla/5.0
            (iPhone; U; CPU iPhone OS 4_0 like Mac OS X; en-us)
            AppleWebKit/532.9 (KHTML, like Gecko) Version/4.0.5
            Mobile/8A293 Safari/6531.22.7");

        FirefoxDriver driver = new FirefoxDriver(profile);
        driver.get("http://www.google.com");
    }
}
```

In the preceding code for the setPreference() method, general.useragent. override is sent as the name of the preference, and the second parameter is the value for that preference, which represents the iPhone user agent. Now open the user.js file for this particular Firefox instance, and you will see the entry for this preference. You should use the following preference in your user.js file:

```
user_pref("general.useragent.override", "Mozilla/5.0 (iPhone; U;
    CPU iPhone OS 4_0 like Mac OS X; en-us) AppleWebKit/532.9
    (KHTML, like Gecko) Version/4.0.5 Mobile/8A293
    Safari/6531.22.7");
```

Apart from this, you will observe that the mobile version of the Google Search page has been served to you.

Understanding frozen preferences

Now, let's go back to the big list of frozen preferences that `user.js` contains, which we have seen earlier. The Firefox Driver thinks that a test script developer doesn't have to deal with them and doesn't allow those values to be changed. Let us pick one frozen preference and try to change its values in our code. Let's consider the preference `browser.shell.checkDefaultBrowser`, whose value FirefoxDriver implementers thought should be set to `false` so that the Firefox browser does not ask you whether to make Firefox your default browser, if it is not already, while you are busy executing your test cases. Ultimately, you don't have to deal with the pop up itself in your test scripts. Apart from setting the preference value to `false`, the implementers of FirefoxDriver also thought of freezing this value so that users don't alter these values. That is the reason these preferences are called frozen preferences. Now, what happens if you try to modify these values in your test scripts? Let's see a code example:

```java
public class FrozenPreferences {
    public static void main(String... args){
        FirefoxProfile profile = new FirefoxProfile();
        profile.setPreference("browser.shell.checkDefaultBrowser", true);

        FirefoxDriver driver = new FirefoxDriver(profile);
        driver.get("http://www.google.com");

    }
}
```

Now when you execute your code, you will immediately see an exception saying you're not allowed to override these values. The following is the exception stack trace you will see:

```
Exception in thread "main" java.lang.IllegalArgumentException: Preference browser.shell.checkDefaultBrowser may not be overridden;
frozen value=false, requested value=true
    at com.google.common.base.Preconditions.checkArgument(Preconditions.java:119)
    at org.openqa.selenium.firefox.Preferences.checkPreference(Preferences.java:223)
    at org.openqa.selenium.firefox.Preferences.setPreference(Preferences.java:156)
    at org.openqa.selenium.firefox.FirefoxProfile.setPreference(FirefoxProfile.java:228)
    at com.packt.webdriver.chapter4.FrozenPreferences.main(FrozenPreferences.java:9)
```

This is how FirefoxDriver mandates a few preferences that are not to be touched. However, there are a few preferences of our frozen list, which FirefoxDriver allows to alter through code. For that, it explicitly exposes methods in the `FirefoxProfile` class. Those exempted preferences are for dealing with SSL certificates and native events. Here, we will see how we can override the SSL certificates' preferences.

Let's use a code example that tries to override the default Firefox behavior to handle SSL certificates. The FirefoxProfile class has two methods to handle the SSL certificates; the first one is as follows:

```
public void setAcceptUntrustedCertificates(boolean
    acceptUntrustedSsl)
```

This lets Firefox know whether to accept SSL certificates that are untrusted. By default, it is set to true, that is, Firefox accepts SSL certificates that are untrusted.

The second method is as follows:

```
public void setAssumeUntrustedCertificateIssuer(boolean
    untrustedIssuer)
```

This lets Firefox assume that the untrusted certificates are issued by untrusted or self-signed certification agents. Firefox, by default, assumes the issuer to be untrusted. That assumption is particularly useful when you test an application in the test environment while using the certificate from the production environment.

The preferences, webdriver_accept_untrusted_certs and webdriver_assume_ untrusted_issuer, are the ones related to the SSL certificates. Now, let us create a Java code to modify the values for these two values. By default, the values are set to true, as seen in the user.js file. Let's mark them as false with the following code:

```
public class SSLCertificatesPreferences {

   public static void main(String... args){
     FirefoxProfile profile = new FirefoxProfile();
     profile.setAssumeUntrustedCertificateIssuer(false);
     profile.setAcceptUntrustedCertificates(false);

     FirefoxDriver driver = new FirefoxDriver(profile);
     driver.get("http://www.google.com");
   }
}
```

Here, we have set the values to false, and now if we open the user.js file in the profile directory of this instance of Firefox, you will see the values set to false, as follows:

```
user_pref("webdriver_accept_untrusted_certs", false);
user_pref("webdriver_assume_untrusted_issuer", false);
```

Similarly, FirefoxDriver enables native events to be invoked in the Firefox browser by exposing a method named `setEnableNativeEvents()`. Using this method, you can override the preference `webdriver_enable_native_events` in the `user.js` file.

Firefox binary

Imagine a situation where you have to test your web application against two different versions of the Firefox browser. By default, when you instantiate FirefoxDriver, the Firefox version that is available on the `PATH` variable is launched. But if you want to launch a different version of Firefox, we need to use Firefox Binary.

Installing multiple versions of Firefox

Now that you have Firefox 17.0.1 version on your machine, let's install Firefox 23.0 version on your system by performing the following steps:

1. Download this version from Mozilla and start installing it.

2. When you reach the following screen in your installation, select **Custom**.

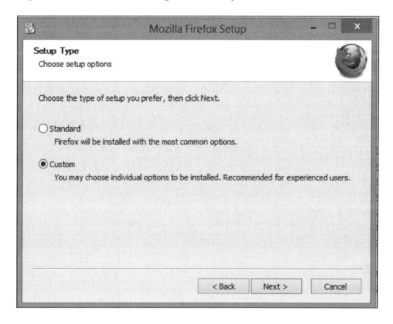

3. Enter the path as `C:\Mozilla Firefox\` in the path field as shown as follows, and proceed with the installation:

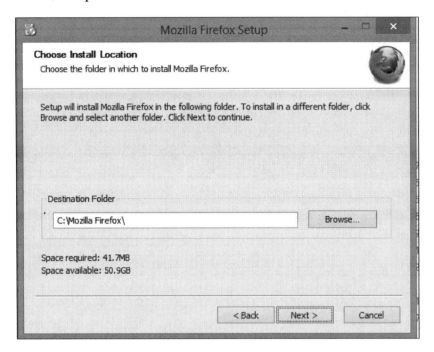

4. Now try to launch Firefox from your code; it will launch Firefox 17.0.1 as it is available in the PATH variable.

5. So, in order to use Firefox 23.0, try to use Firefox Binary. The following is the code example for it:

```
public class MultipleFirefoxBinaries {
  public static void main(String... args){
    FirefoxBinary binary = new FirefoxBinary(new
      File("C:\\Mozilla Firefox\\firefox.exe"));
    FirefoxProfile profile = new FirefoxProfile();

    FirefoxDriver driver = new FirefoxDriver(binary, profile);
    driver.get("http://www.google.com");
  }
}
```

In the preceding code, the first line of the main function instantiates the `FirefoxBinary` class by providing the path to the `firefox.exe` file that launches Firefox 23.0. The API syntax for the constructor is as follows:

```
publicFirefoxBinary(java.io.File pathToFirefoxBinary)
```

Here, the input parameter is a file whose path is set to the `firefox.exe` file of the targeted version.

Now, we have to use one of the overloaded versions of the FirefoxDriver constructor, which takes `FirefoxBinary` and `FirefoxProfile` as the input parameters to instantiate as shown in preceding code. When executed, the preceding code should launch Firefox 23.0. Navigate to **Help | About Firefox** to arrive at the following screenshot:

InternetExplorerDriver

In order to execute your test scripts on the Internet Explorer browser, you need WebDriver's InternetExplorerDriver.

Installing InternetExplorerDriver

IEDriver server can be downloaded from `https://code.google.com/p/selenium/downloads/list`.

The following are the sequence of steps you need to perform to install the driver:

1. Download the 32-bit or 64-bit version based on the Internet Explorer that is installed on your computer.

2. Unzip the file and you will see the `IEDriverServer.exe` file.

3. Double-click on the file to launch WebDriver's InternetExplorerDriver as a
    service that listens on a port shown as follows:

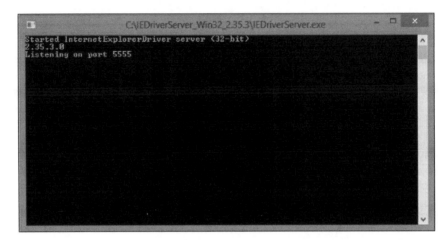

Here, the InternetExplorerDriver is running as the service on port 5555.

4. Start your server, and it might start on a different random port. Now point
    your browser to http://localhost:5555/status and it will return the
    details of the IE Server as JSON in the following manner:

```
{
    "sessionId": "",
    "status": 0,
    "value": {
        "build": {
            "version": "2.35.3.0"
        },
        "os": {
            "arch": "x86",
            "name": "windows",
            "version": "6.2.9200"
        }
    }
}
```

Until now, you have started IEDriver as a service that listens on a port and can
be communicated over HTTP. Your client library constructs all your test script
commands as JSON and hands it over to the IEDriver server. This again confers
to JSONWireProtocol. The IEDriver server then uses its IEThreadExplorer class,
which is written in C++, to drive the IE browser using the Component Object Model
framework.

Writing your first test script for the IE browser

Now you are all set to write test scripts that run on the Internet Explorer browser. The following is the code that instantiates InternetExplorerDriver:

```
import org.openqa.selenium.WebDriver;
import org.openqa.selenium.ie.InternetExplorerDriver;

public class UsingIEDriver {
  public static void main(String... args) {
    WebDriver driver = new InternetExplorerDriver();
    driver.get("http://www.google.com");
  }
}
```

On the first line in the main method, we have created an instance of InternetExplorerDriver. But when you try to execute the code, you will see an exception thrown from the driver code as follows:

```
Exception in thread "main" java.lang.IllegalStateException: The path to the driver executable
must be set by the webdriver.ie.driver system property; for more information, see http://
code.google.com/p/selenium/wiki/InternetExplorerDriver. The latest version can be
downloaded from http://code.google.com/p/selenium/downloads/list
    at com.google.common.base.Preconditions.checkState(Preconditions.java:176)
```

This is because your InternetExplorerDriver expects your code to specify the location of the `IEDriverServer.exe` file. Before the test case execution starts, IEDriver needs to know the location of `IEDriverServer.exe` to start it as a server on a port.

Now, modify the preceding code to have the location of the server file by setting a system property. It looks as follows:

```
public class UsingIEDriver {

  public static void main(String... args) {
    System.setProperty("webdriver.ie.driver",
      "C:\\IEDriverServer_Win32_2.35.3\\IEDriverServer.exe");

    WebDriver driver = new InternetExplorerDriver();
    driver.get("http://www.google.com");
  }
}
```

If you are wondering where you can find the list of all the properties, here is the location: `http://selenium.googlecode.com/git/docs/api/java/constant-values.html#org.openqa.selenium.ie.InternetExplorerDriver.NATIVE_EVENTS`.

So, by setting that, InternetExplorerDriver knows the location of the server file and starts the server. The following is the output message of the server that has started on port 18873. But you will still see another exception being thrown by IEDriver, as shown in the following screenshot:

```
Started InternetExplorerDriver server (32-bit)
2.35.3.0
Listening on port 18873

Exception in thread main org.openqa.selenium.remote.SessionNotFoundException: Unexpected error launc
hing Internet Explorer.
Protected Mode settings are not the same for all zones.
Enable Protected Mode must be set to the same value (enabled or disabled) for all zones.
(WARNING: The server did not provide any stacktrace information)
Command duration or timeout: 1.25 seconds
Build info: version: '2.33.0', revision: '4e90c97', time: '2013-05-22 15:33:32'
System info: os.name: 'Windows 8', os.arch: 'x86', os.version: '6.2', java.version: '1.7.0_21'
Driver info: org.openqa.selenium.ie.InternetExplorerDriver
    at sun.reflect.NativeConstructorAccessorImpl.newInstance0(Native Method)
    at sun.reflect.NativeConstructorAccessorImpl.newInstance(Unknown Source)
    at sun.reflect.DelegatingConstructorAccessorImpl.newInstance(Unknown Source)
    at java.lang.reflect.Constructor.newInstance(Unknown Source)
    at org.openqa.selenium.remote.ErrorHandler.createThrowable(ErrorHandler.java:191)
    at com.packt.webdriver.chapter4.UsingIEDriver.main(UsingIEDriver.java:16)
```

Here, the driver talks about the Protected Mode settings of the IE browser for different zones. The reason behind it, in the very own words of developers of IEDriver, is stated at http://code.google.com/r/bookie988-wiki-modifications/source/browse/InternetExplorerDriverInternals.wiki.

IE7 on Windows Vista introduced the concept of Protected Mode, which allows for some measure of protection to the underlying Windows OS when browsing. The problem is that when you manipulate an instance of IE via COM, and navigate to a page that would cause a transition into or out of Protected Mode, IE requires that another browser session be created. This will orphan the COM object of the previous session, not allowing you to control it any longer.

In IE7, this will usually manifest itself as a new top-level browser window; in IE8, a new IExplore.exe process will be created, but it will usually (not always!) seamlessly attach it to the existing IE top-level frame window. Any browser automation framework that drives IE externally (as opposed to using a WebBrowser control) will run into these problems.

In order to work around that problem, IEDriver dictates that to work with IE, all zones must have the same Protected Mode setting. As long as it's on for all zones or off for all zones, IEDriver can prevent the transitions to different Protected Mode zones that would invalidate the IEDriver's browser object. It also allows users to continue to run with the user account controls turned on and to run securely in the browser if they set Protected Mode on for all zones.

In earlier releases of the IE Driver, if the user's Protected Mode settings were not correctly set, it would launch IE, and the process would simply hang until the HTTP request timed out. This was suboptimal, as it gave no indication about what needed to be set. Erring on the side of caution, IE Driver does not modify the user's Protected Mode settings. Current versions, however, check that the Protected Mode settings are properly set, and return an error response if they are not.

Now, open your IE browser and go to **Tools | Internet Options | Security**. The following are the screenshots of settings for the four different security zones. If you observe, the **Enable Protected Mode** is unchecked for the **Local Intranet** zone in my settings, although it is checked for the rest of the three zones. You might have different settings.

Now, check the **Local Intranet** option as well and rerun the preceding Java test script. Your IEDriver should launch the IE browser successfully and bring in the Google Search page. Congratulations! You have executed your first code to launch the IE browser.

Having done that, you may not be able to check and modify your browser security settings every time you execute your test scripts. To deal with this, IEDriver gives you an option to ignore these security domains. Setting this option as a desired capability will solve the problem. The following is the code to do that:

```
public class UsingIEDriver {

  public static void main(String... args) {
    System.setProperty("webdriver.ie.driver",
    "C:\\IEDriverServer_Win32_2.35.3\\IEDriverServer.exe");
    DesiredCapabilities ieCapabilities =
    DesiredCapabilities.internetExplorer();

    ieCapabilities.setCapability(InternetExplorerDriver.INTRODUCE_
FLAKINE
      SS_BY_IGNORING_SECURITY_DOMAINS,
      true);
    WebDriver driver = new InternetExplorerDriver(ieCapabilities);
    driver.get("http://www.google.com");
  }
}
```

Building the InternetExplorer driver service

The IEDriver server provides a way for the test script developer to configure it; that is, the port it should run on, the location where the temporary files should be extracted, and so on via the client library. The `InternetExplorerDriverService.Builder` class can be used to achieve this. Let us see how we can do that. Currently, every time you execute your `UsingIEDriver.java` class, the IEDriverServer is started on a different random port. Suppose you want to make sure your server always started on the same port, you can do that using this builder class. Similarly, if you want to execute your tests pointing to an IEDriver server running on a different machine, you can do that as well by pointing to the machine's IP address. Let's see how to achieve that in the following code:

```
public class BuildingIEDriverService {
  public static void main(String... args){
    System.setProperty("webdriver.ie.driver",
```

```
            "C:\\IEDriverServer_Win32_2.35.3\\IEDriverServer.exe");

    InternetExplorerDriverService.Builder builder
        = new InternetExplorerDriverService.Builder();

    InternetExplorerDriverService srvc =
        builder.usingPort(5555).withHost("127.0.0.1").build();

    DesiredCapabilities ieCapabilities = DesiredCapabilities
        .internetExplorer();
    ieCapabilities.setCapability(

    InternetExplorerDriver.INTRODUCE_FLAKINESS_BY_IGNORING_SECURITY_DO
    MAINS,true);


    WebDriver driver = new InternetExplorerDriver(srvc,
        ieCapabilities);
    driver.get("http://www.google.com");
    }
}
```

The highlighted lines of the preceding code is where we have created an instance of the `InternetExplorerDriverService` builder class and used the builder design pattern to assign a port 5555 and a host IP 127.0.0.1, which is the localhost here, as we run the driver on the same machine as the service. Now, when you start executing this code, the code initially starts the IEDriver service on the port and starts executing your test commands onto that server. The output of the preceding code execution will be as follows:

```
Started InternetExplorerDriver server (32-bit)
2.35.3.0
Listening on port 5555
Bound to network adapter with IP address 127.0.0.1
```

Open your task manager of Windows OS, and you will see the IEDriver Server process running, as shown in the following screenshot:

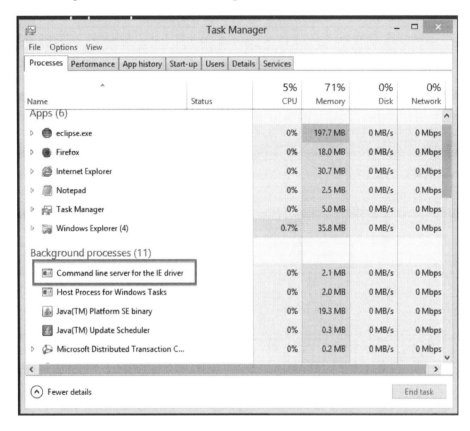

Now if you reexecute your code, you will not be able to start your IEDriver server, because it's already started and is running on that port. So, your test case will result in the following error:

Failed to start the server with: port = '5555', host = '127.0.0.1', log level = ", log file = "

So, before reexecuting your test case, end the IEDriver server process in the task manager and rerun your test case. It should work fine. But it will be highly inconvenient to do this process manually every time before you execute your test case. This is the reason your WebDriver client library has an inbuilt method called `quit()` to do it for you.

The API syntax is as follows:

```
void quit()
```

This will kill the driver, driver's server, and all associated browser windows for you. Modify your `BuildingIEDriverService` class to have this method at the end shown as follows, and try executing it several times. Your test script should be executed without any failures irrespective of the number of times you execute it.

```
public class BuildingIEDriverService {
  public static void main(String... args){
    System.setProperty("webdriver.ie.driver",
      "C:\\IEDriverServer_Win32_2.35.3\\IEDriverServer.exe");

    InternetExplorerDriverService.Builder builder
      = new InternetExplorerDriverService.Builder();

    InternetExplorerDriverService srvc =
      builder.usingPort(5555).withHost("127.0.0.1").build();

    DesiredCapabilities ieCapabilities = DesiredCapabilities
      .internetExplorer();
    ieCapabilities.setCapability(
      InternetExplorerDriver.INTRODUCE_FLAKINESS_BY_IGNORING_SECURITY_
DO
      MAINS, true);

    WebDriver driver = new InternetExplorerDriver(srvc,
      ieCapabilities);
    driver.get("http://www.google.com");
    driver.quit();
  }
}
```

But if you want to just stop the IEDriver server and not close the associated browser windows, you can invoke `stop()` on the InternetExplorerDriverService. Add the following code instead of `driver.quit()` to the preceding code and reexecute it:

```
srvc.stop();
```

Understanding IEDriver capabilities

In this section, we will discuss some of the important capabilities of InternetExplorerDriver. In the two preceding test scripts, we have seen how to use DesiredCapabilities. That is where we have set the IEDriver capability to ignore the security domains. The code is as follows:

```
DesiredCapabilities ieCapabilities = DesiredCapabilities
    .internetExplorer();
ieCapabilities.setCapability(InternetExplorerDriver.INTRODUCE_FLAK
    INESS_BY_IGNORING_SECURITY_DOMAINS,true);
```

Similar to INTRODUCE_FLAKINESS_BY_IGNORING_SECURITY_DOMAINS, IEDriver has many other capabilities. The following is a list of those with an explanation on why it is used:

Capability	Value to be Set	Purpose
INITIAL_BROWSER_URL	URL, for example, http://www.google.com	This capability is set with the URL value that the driver should navigate the browser to as soon as it opens up.
INTRODUCE_FLAKINESS_BY_IGNORING_SECURITY_DOMAINS	True or False	This defines if the IEDriverServer should ignore the browser security domain settings.
NATIVE_EVENTS	True or False	This tells the IEDriver server whether to use native events or JavaScript events for executing mouse or keyboard actions.
REQUIRE_WINDOW_FOCUS	True or False	If the value is set to True, the IE browser window will get the focus. This is especially useful when executing native events.
ENABLE_PERSISTENT_HOVERING	True or False	If set to True, IEDriver will persistently fire a mouse-hovering event. This is especially important to overcome issues with how IE handles mouse-over events.
IE_ENSURE_CLEAN_SESSION	True or False	If True, it clears all the cookies, cache, history, and saved form data of all the instances of IE.
IE_SET_PROXY_BY_SERVER	True or False	If True, the proxy server set for the IEDriver server is used. If False, WindowsProxyManager is used to determine the proxy server.

ChromeDriver

ChromeDriver, to some extent, is similar to IEDriver in the way it works. It has three components to it: the first is the client language bindings, the second is the Chrome browser itself, and the third is the Chrome Driver Server that sits in between the language bindings and the Chrome browser.

Installing ChromeDriver

The following are the sequence of steps to install ChromeDriver:

1. Download the ChromeDriver Server installable from `http://` `chromedriver.storage.googleapis.com/index.html`, and download the server that is appropriate for your OS platform.

2. Unzip the file and run the `chromedriver.exe` file if you are on Windows. This should start your ChromeDriver Server on port `9515`, as follows:

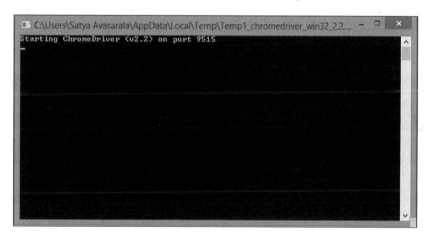

3. Now, if you haven't installed the Chrome browser, it's time to do so. You can install the Chrome browser from `https://www.google.com/intl/en_uk/` `chrome/browser/`.

ChromeDriver, similar to IEDriver, uses JSONWireProtocol to communicate with the Chrome Driver server. It serializes all your test script commands into JSON and sends them over the wire to the Chrome Driver server. The server uses the Chrome's automation proxy framework to control the Chrome browser.

Writing your first test script for the Chrome browser

Let us bring on our standard Google Search page using ChromeDriver, as shown in the following code:

```
public class UsingChromeDriver {
  public static void main(String... args){
    System.setProperty("webdriver.chrome.driver",
      "C:\\chromedriver_win32_2.2\\chromedriver.exe");

    WebDriver driver = new ChromeDriver();
    driver.get("http://www.google.com");
    WebElement searchBox = driver.findElement(By.name("q"));
    searchBox.sendKeys("Chrome Driver");
  }
}
```

Here also, you will specify the ChromeDriver server location as a system property. ChromeDriver will launch the server before executing its test commands. In the second line of the main method, an instance of ChromeDriver has been created. The rest is the same as with FirefoxDriver or IEDriver.

If you execute the above code several times, you will see that the port being assigned to the server changes randomly. Similar to the IEDriver server, if you want your ChromeDriver server to use the same port, you can use the ChromeDriverService class as follows:

```
public class BuildingChromeDriverService {
  public static void main(String... args){

//Start the ChromeDriver Server
    System.setProperty("webdriver.chrome.driver",
      "C:\\chromedriver_win32_2.2\\chromedriver.exe");

  ChromeDriverService.Builder builder =  new
    ChromeDriverService.Builder();
  ChromeDriverService srvc = builder.usingDriverExecutable(new
    File("C:\\chromedriver_win32_2.2\\chromedriver.exe"))
  .usingPort(65423).build();
  try {
    srvc.start();
  } catch (IOException e) {
    e.printStackTrace();
  }
```

```
        //Execute your test-script commands
        WebDriver driver = new ChromeDriver(srvc);
        driver.get("http://www.google.com");
        WebElement searchBox = driver.findElement(By.name("q"));
        searchBox.sendKeys("Chrome Driver");

        //Stop the Server
        driver.quit();
        srvc.stop();

    }
}
```

The whole implementation is exactly like what we have done for the InternetExplorerDriver server.

Using ChromeOptions

ChromeOptions are similar to Firefox profiles. You can add extensions to your Chrome browser, specify the binary location of the Chrome browser if you have multiple versions of Chrome browsers installed on your machine, and so on. In this section, we will see how we can use ChromeOptions to add an extension.

The `UsingChromeOptions` class is as follows:

```
public class UsingChromeOptions {
  public static void main(String... args){
    //Start the ChromeDriver Server
    System.setProperty("webdriver.chrome.driver",
      "C:\\chromedriver_win32_2.2\\chromedriver.exe");
    ChromeDriverService.Builder builder =  new
      ChromeDriverService.Builder();
    ChromeDriverService srvc = builder.usingDriverExecutable(new
      File("C:\\chromedriver_win32_2.2\\chromedriver.exe"))

    .usingPort(65423).build();
    try {
      srvc.start();
    } catch (IOException e) {
      e.printStackTrace();
    }

    // Chrome Options
    ChromeOptions opts = new ChromeOptions();
```

```
opts.addExtensions(new File("C:\\firebug.crx"));

//Execute your test-script commands
WebDriver driver = new ChromeDriver(srvc, opts);
driver.get("http://www.google.com");
WebElement searchBox = driver.findElement(By.name("q"));
searchBox.sendKeys("Chrome Driver");
    }
}
```

The highlighted code is where we have added the `Firebug.crx` file, which is a Chrome extension file. Now, you will see the firebug extension added to your browser as follows:

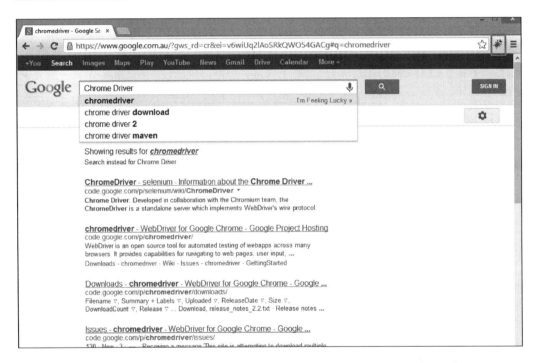

Similarly, you can use Chrome options to add more extensions, arguments, and Binaries to your Chrome browser.

SafariDriver

SafariDriver is implemented as an extension to the Safari browser. SafariDriver communicates with this extension using web sockets, which is slightly different in implementation from the rest of the WebDrivers. SafariDriver comes bundled default with the `Selenium.jar` file just as with FirefoxDriver. You do not have to download it separately.

As I've mentioned earlier, the Safari Driver is implemented as an extension to the Safari browser. This extension comprises of the following three different components:

- **Global Extension**: This is the component of the extension that talks to the external world; that is, to the WebDriver client bindings. This is loaded when the Safari browser is first launched, and injects a script into every web page that is loaded onto the Safari browser. This also maintains a record of all the Safari browser windows opened. Global extensions talks to the client bindings using web sockets.

- **Injected Script**: This script is injected into the web page loaded on the browser, and it is primarily responsible for executing all your test script commands. The injected scripts talks to the global extension using `SafariContentBrowsertabProxy`, while Global Extension talks to the injected script using `SafariWebPageProxy`.

- **Page Script**: This is an extra script injected as a tag by the above injected script, each time it is loaded. While the injected script handles most of the client commands, this script takes care of some of the commands that are executed in the page's context. The page script communicates with the injected script using `window.postMessage`.

Writing your first test script for the Safari browser

This is as straightforward as FirefoxDriver. Download and install the Safari browser, if you haven't done already. The following is the test script using the Safari Driver:

```
public class UsingSafariDriver {
  public static void main(String... args){
    System.setProperty("SafariDefaultPath",
      "C:\\Safari\\Safari.exe");
    WebDriver driver = new SafariDriver();
    driver.get("http://www.google.com");
    driver.findElement(By.name("q")).sendKeys("Packt Publishing");
```

```
        driver.findElement(By.name("btnG")).click();
        driver.quit();
    }
}
```

In your test script, you have to mention the path to the Safari browser executable to be launched. Otherwise, you can set it in the system's PATH variable. From there on, your test script should look the same as the FirefoxDriver test script.

OperaDriver

OperaDriver is, obviously, used to test your application on the Opera browser using WebDriver. OperaDriver is being developed by the Opera software itself. It uses the scope transport protocol to communicate between OperaDriver and the Opera browser.

Installing OperaDriver

The following are the sequence of steps to be performed to install OperaDriver:

1. You need to download the OperaDriver software. It is available at https://github.com/operasoftware/operadriver/downloads. I have downloaded version 1.1.

2. Apart from that, you need to install the Opera browser. Right now, OperaDriver has support only up to the Opera browser 12.x or older. So, try to install the 12 or older version of the Opera browser. You can install older versions at http://arc.opera.com/pub/opera/. We've installed the 12.11 version of the browser.

Writing your first test script for the Opera browser

The following is the first test script that can be used to launch the Google Search page on the Opera browser:

```
public class UsingOperaDriver {
    public static void main(String... args){
        System.setProperty("os.name","windows");
        System.setProperty("opera.binary", "C:\\Program
            Files\\Opera\\opera.exe");
        WebDriver driver = new OperaDriver();
```

```
driver.get("http://www.google.com");
driver.findElement(By.name("q")).sendKeys("Packt Publishing");
driver.findElement(By.name("btnG")).click();
driver.quit();
  }
}
```

You will specify the Binary location and platform name, and the rest should be similar to other drivers.

Summary

In this chapter, you have seen some of the major implementations of WebDriver that are widely used in the industry. The other similar drivers are the Safari Driver and the Opera Driver that work in similar lines. The underlying technology for every driver is JSONWireProtocol, which is fundamental for all the implementations.

In the next chapter, we will learn about the framework that WebDriver provides to deal with keyboard and mouse events.

5
Understanding WebDriver Events

Selenium WebDriver provides a very good framework for tracking the various events that happen while you're executing your test scripts using WebDriver. Many navigation events that get fired before and after an event occurs (such as before and after navigating to a URL, before and after browser back-navigation, and so on) can be tracked and captured. To throw an event, WebDriver gives you a class named EventFiringWebDriver, and to catch that event, it provides the test script developer an interface named WebDriverEventListener. The test script developer should provide their own implementations for the overridden methods from the interface. In this chapter, we will see how we can track various browser navigation events and web element action events that get triggered during the execution of your test cases.

Introducing EventFiringWebDriver and EventListener classes

The EventFiringWebDriver class is a wrapper around your normal WebDriver that gives the driver the capability to fire events. The EventListener class, on the other hand, waits to listen from EventFiringWebDriver and handles all of the events that are dispatched. There can be more than one listener waiting to hear from the EventFiringWebDriver class for an event to fire. All of the event listeners should be registered with the EventFiringWebDriver class to get notified.

The following flow diagram explains what has to be done to capture all of the events raised by EventFiringWebDriver during the execution of test cases:

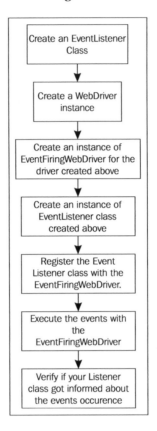

Creating an instance of EventListener

The EventListener class handles all of the events that are dispatched by the EventFiringWebDriver class. There are the following two ways to create an EventListener class:

- By implementing the WebDriverEventListener interface.
- By extending the AbstractWebDriverEventListener class provided in the WebDriver library.

It is up to you, as a test script developer, to choose which way to go by.

Implementing WebDriverEventListener

The WebDriverEventListener interface has all of the event methods declared. The EventFiringWebDriver class, as soon as it realizes an event has occurred, will invoke the registered method of WebDriverEventListener. Here, we have created an IAmTheEventListener named class and have implemented WebDriverEventListener. As a result, you have to provide implementations for all of the methods declared in it. Right now, in WebDriverEventListener, there are 15 methods. We will discuss each one of them shortly. For now, make sure you allow your Eclipse IDE to provide you dummy implementations for all of these methods. The class that we have created with all 15 overridden methods is as follows (we have provided implementations for couple of methods):

```java
public class IAmTheEventListener implements WebDriverEventListener{

////////// NAVIGATION RELATED METHODS //////////////////
    @Override
    public void beforeNavigateTo(String url, WebDriver driver) {
        System.out.println("Before Navigate To "+url);

    }

    @Override
    public void afterNavigateTo(String url, WebDriver driver) {
        // TODO Auto-generated method stub

    }

    @Override
    public void beforeNavigateBack(WebDriver driver) {
        System.out.println("Before Navigate Back. Right now I'm at
"+driver.getCurrentUrl());

    }

    @Override
    public void afterNavigateBack(WebDriver driver) {
        // TODO Auto-generated method stub

    }

    @Override
    public void beforeNavigateForward(WebDriver driver) {
        // TODO Auto-generated method stub

    }

    @Override
```

```java
    public void afterNavigateForward(WebDriver driver) {
        // TODO Auto-generated method stub

    }

////////////////// FINDBY RELATED METHODS //////////////
    @Override
    public void beforeFindBy(By by, WebElement element, WebDriver
driver) {
        // TODO Auto-generated method stub

    }

    @Override
    public void afterFindBy(By by, WebElement element, WebDriver
driver) {
        // TODO Auto-generated method stub

    }

////////////////// CLICKON RELATED METHODS //////////////
    @Override
    public void beforeClickOn(WebElement element, WebDriver driver) {
        // TODO Auto-generated method stub

    }

    @Override
    public void afterClickOn(WebElement element, WebDriver driver) {
        // TODO Auto-generated method stub

    }

////////////////// CHANGE OF VALUE RELATED METHODS //////////////
    @Override
    public void beforeChangeValueOf(WebElement element, WebDriver
driver) {
        // TODO Auto-generated method stub

    }

    @Override
    public void afterChangeValueOf(WebElement element, WebDriver
driver) {
        // TODO Auto-generated method stub

    }

////////////////// SCRIPT EXECUTION RELATED METHODS //////////////
    @Override
```

```
public void beforeScript(String script, WebDriver driver) {
    // TODO Auto-generated method stub

}

@Override
public void afterScript(String script, WebDriver driver) {
    // TODO Auto-generated method stub

}

////////////// EXCEPTION RELATED METHODS /////////////////////////
@Override
public void onException(Throwable throwable, WebDriver driver) {
    // TODO Auto-generated method stub

}

}
```

Extending AbstractWebDriverEventListener

The second way to create a listener class is by extending the
AbstractWebDriverEventListener class. AbstractWebDriverEventListener
is an abstract class that implements WebDriverEventListener. Though it doesn't
really provide any implementation for the methods in the WebDriverEventListener
interface, it creates a dummy implementation such that the listener class that you are
creating doesn't have to contain all of the methods; only the ones that you, as a test
script developer, are interested. The following is a class we have created that extends
AbstractWebDriverEventListener and provides implementations for a couple
of methods in it. This way we can override only the methods that we are interested
rather than all of the methods in our class:

```
public class IAmTheEventListener2 extends
AbstractWebDriverEventListener{

    @Override
    public void beforeNavigateTo(String url, WebDriver driver) {
        System.out.println("Before Navigate To "+url);

    }

    @Override
    public void beforeNavigateBack(WebDriver driver) {
        System.out.println("Before Navigate Back. Right now I'm at
"+driver.getCurrentUrl());

    }
}
```

Creating a WebDriver instance

Now that we have created our listener class that listens for all of the events generated, it's time to create our test script class and let it call IAmTheDriver.java. After you create the class, create a FirefoxDriver instance in it:

```
WebDriver driver = new FirefoxDriver();
```

The FirefoxDriver instance will be the underlying driver instance that drives all of your driver events. This is nothing new compared to what we have done until now in all of the chapters in this book. The step explained in the next section is where we make this driver an instance of EventFiringWebDriver.

Creating EventFiringWebDriver and EventListener instances

Now that we have the basic driver instance, pass it as an argument while constructing the EventFiringWebDriver instance. We will be using this instance of the driver to execute all of the further user actions.

Now, using the following code, instantiate the EventListener, IAmTheEventListener.java, or IAmTheEventListener2.java classes that we created previously. This will be the class to which all of the events are dispatched:

```
EventFiringWebDriver eventFiringDriver
        = new EventFiringWebDriver(driver);
    IAmTheEventListener eventListener = new IAmTheEventListener();
```

Registering EventListener with EventFiringWebDriver

In order for the event executions to be notified to EventListener, we have registered EventListener to the EventFiringWebDriver class. Now the EventFiringWebDriver class will know where to send the notifications. This is done as shown in the following line of code:

```
eventFiringDriver.register(eventListener);
```

Executing and verifying the events

Now it's time for our test script to execute events such as navigation events. Let's first navigate to Google and then Facebook. Now, we will use the browser back-navigation to go back to Google. The full code of the test script is as follows:

```
public class IAmTheDriver {
    public static void main(String... args){
        WebDriver driver = new FirefoxDriver();

        EventFiringWebDriver eventFiringDriver = new
EventFiringWebDriver(driver);
        IAmTheEventListener eventListener = new IAmTheEventListener();
        eventFiringDriver.register(eventListener);

        eventFiringDriver.get("http://www.google.com");
        eventFiringDriver.get("http://www.facebook.com");
        eventFiringDriver.navigate().back();

    }
}
```

In the preceding code, we modify our listener class to record `navigateTo` and `navigateBack` before and after events inherited from the `AbstractWebDriverEventListener` class. The modified methods are as follows:

```
@Override
public void beforeNavigateTo(String url, WebDriver driver) {
    System.out.println("Before Navigate To: "+url
            +" and Current url is: "+driver.getCurrentUrl());

}

@Override
public void afterNavigateTo(String url, WebDriver driver) {
    System.out.println("After Navigate To: "+url
            +" and Current url is: "+driver.getCurrentUrl());

}

@Override
public void beforeNavigateBack(WebDriver driver) {
    System.out.println("Before Navigate Back. Right now I'm at "
                +driver.getCurrentUrl());

}
```

```
    @Override
    public void afterNavigateBack(WebDriver driver) {
        System.out.println("After Navigate Back. Right now I'm at "
                +driver.getCurrentUrl());

    }
```

Now, if you execute your test script, the output will be as follows:

```
Before Navigate To: http://www.google.com and Current url is: about:blank
After Navigate To: http://www.google.com and Current url is: https://www.google.com.au/
Before Navigate To: http://www.facebook.com and Current url is: https://www.google.com.au/
After Navigate To: http://www.facebook.com and Current url is: https://www.facebook.com/
Before Navigate Back. Right now I'm at https://www.facebook.com/
After Navigate Back. Right now I'm at https://www.google.com.au/
```

If you observe the second line in the previously shown output, the expected after-navigation URL is http://www.google.com, but the current URL is http://www.google.com.au. This is due to Google redirection to your local server.

Registering multiple EventListeners

We can register more than one listener with EventFiringWebDriver. Once the event occurs, all of the registered listeners are notified about it. Let's modify our test script as follows to register both our IAmTheListener.java and IAmTheListener2.java files:

```
public class RegisteringMultipleListeners {
    public static void main(String... args){

        WebDriver driver = new FirefoxDriver();
        EventFiringWebDriver eventFiringDriver = new
EventFiringWebDriver(driver);
        IAmTheEventListener eventListener = new IAmTheEventListener();
        IAmTheEventListener2 eventListener2 = new
IAmTheEventListener2();

        eventFiringDriver.register(eventListener);
        eventFiringDriver.register(eventListener2);

        eventFiringDriver.get("http://www.google.com");
        eventFiringDriver.get("http://www.facebook.com");

        eventFiringDriver.navigate().back();
    }
}
```

Now, modify the listeners slightly to differentiate the log statements. Now, if you execute the preceding code, you will see the output as follows:

```
IAmTheEventListener: Before Navigate To: http://www.google.com and Current url is: about:blank
IAmTheEventListener2: Before Navigate To: http://www.google.com and Current url is: about:blank
IAmTheEventListener: After Navigate To: http://www.google.com and Current url is: https://www.google.com.au/
IAmTheEventListener2: After Navigate To: http://www.google.com and Current url is: https://www.google.com.au/
IAmTheEventListener: Before Navigate To: http://www.facebook.com and Current url is: https://www.google.com.au/
IAmTheEventListener2: Before Navigate To: http://www.facebook.com and Current url is: https://www.google.com.au/
IAmTheEventListener: After Navigate To: http://www.facebook.com and Current url is: https://www.facebook.com/
IAmTheEventListener2: After Navigate To: http://www.facebook.com and Current url is: https://www.facebook.com/
IAmTheEventListener: Before Navigate Back. Right now I'm at https://www.facebook.com/
IAmTheEventListener2: Before Navigate Back. Right now I'm at https://www.facebook.com/
IAmTheEventListener: After Navigate Back. Right now I'm at https://www.google.com.au/
IAmTheEventListener2: After Navigate Back. Right now I'm at https://www.google.com.au/
```

Exploring different WebDriver event listeners

We have seen some of the methods in our `EventListeners` that get invoked when their corresponding events are executed, for example, before and after navigation methods are invoked when the `navigateTo` event is triggered. Here we'll see all of the methods that `WebDriverEventListener` provides us.

Listening for WebElement value change

This event occurs when the value of a WebElement changes when the `sendKeys()` or `clear()` methods are executed on them. There are two methods associated with this event.

```
public void beforeChangeValueOf(WebElement element, WebDriver driver)
```

The preceding method is invoked before the WebDriver attempts to change the value of the WebElement. As a parameter, the WebElement itself is passed to the method so that you can log the value of the element before the change.

```
public void afterChangeValueOf(WebElement element,
WebDriver driver)
```

The preceding method is the second method associated with the value-change event that is invoked after the driver changes the value of the WebElement. Again, the WebElement and the WebDriver are sent as parameters to the method. If an exception occurs while changing the value, this method is not invoked.

Listening for WebElement clicked

This event occurs when a WebElement is clicked, that is by executing `webElement.click()`. There are two methods to listen for this event in the `WebDriverEventListener` implementation.

```
public void beforeClickOn(WebElement element, WebDriver driver)
```

The preceding method is invoked when the WebDriver is about to click on a particular WebElement. The WebElement that is going to be clicked on and the WebDriver that is clicking on it are sent as parameters to this method so that the test script developer can interpret which driver performed the click action, and on which element the action was performed.

```
public void afterClickOn(WebElement element, WebDriver driver)
```

The `EventFiringWebDriver` class notifies the preceding method after the click action is taken on a WebElement. Similar to the `beforeClickOn()` method, this method is also sent the WebElement and WebDriver instances. If an exception occurs during a click event, this method is not called.

Listening for a WebElement search event

This event is triggered when the WebDriver searches for a WebElement on the webpage using `findElement()` or `findElements()`. There are, again, two methods associated for this event.

```
public void beforeFindBy(By by, WebElement element, WebDriver driver)
```

The preceding method is invoked just before WebDriver begins searching for a particular WebElement on the page. For parameters, it sends the locating mechanism, that is, the WebElement that is searched for and the WebDriver instance that is performing the search, by instance.

```
public void afterFindBy(By by, WebElement element, WebDriver driver)
```

Similarly, the `EventFiringWebDriver` class calls the preceding method after the search for an element is over and the element is found. If there are any exceptions during the search, this method is not called, and an exception is raised.

Listening for browser back navigation

The browser back navigation event, as we have already seen, gets invoked when we use the `driver.navigation().back()` method. The browser goes back one level in its history. Just as all other events, this event is associated with two methods.

```
public void beforeNavigateBack(WebDriver driver)
```

The preceding method is invoked before the browser takes you back in its history. The WebDriver that invoked this event is passed as a parameter to this method.

```
public void afterNavigateBack(WebDriver driver)
```

Just as in all after <<event>> methods, the preceding method is invoked when the navigate-back action is triggered. The preceding two methods will be invoked irrespective of the navigation of the browser; that is, if the browser doesn't have any history and you invoke this method, the browser doesn't take you to any of its history. But even in that case, as the event is triggered, those two methods are invoked.

Listening for browser forward navigation

This event is very similar to the browser back navigation, except that this is browser forward navigation, that is using, `driver.navigate().forward()`. The two methods associated with this event are as follows:

- `public void afterNavigateForward(WebDriver driver)`
- `public void beforeNavigateForward(WebDriver driver)`

Just as in browser back navigation, these methods are invoked irrespective of whether or not the browser takes you one level forward.

Listening for browser navigateTo events

As we've seen earlier, this event occurs whenever the driver executes `driver.get(url)`. The related methods for this event are as follows:

- `public void beforeNavigateTo(java.lang.String url, WebDriver driver)`
- `public void afterNavigateTo(java.lang.String url, WebDriver driver)`

The URL that is used for the driver navigation is passed as a parameter to the preceding methods along with the driver that triggered the event.

Listening for script execution

This event is triggered whenever the driver executes a JavaScript. The associated methods for this event are as follows:

- `public void beforeScript(java.lang.String script, WebDriver driver)`
- `public void afterScript(java.lang.String script, WebDriver driver)`

The preceding methods get the JavaScript that was executed as a string, and the WebDriver that executed it as a parameter. If there an exception occurs during script execution, the `afterScript()` method will not be invoked.

Listening for any exception

This event occurs when the WebDriver comes across some exceptions. For instance, if you try to search for a WebElement using `findElement()`, and that element doesn't exist on the page, the driver throws an exception (`NoSuchElementException`). At this point, this event is triggered, and the following method gets notified:

```
public void onException(java.lang.Throwable throwable, WebDriver
driver)
```

In all the `after<<event>>` methods, we have seen that they will not be invoked if the driver comes across any exception. In that case, instead of those `after<<events>>` methods, the `onException()` method is invoked and the throwable object and the WebDriver object are sent to it as parameters.

Unregistering EventListener with EventFiringWebDriver

Now, we have seen the different kinds of events that get triggered, and the `EventFiringWebDriver` class notifying all of the listeners registered to it. If, at any point, you want one of your event listeners to stop hearing from `EventFiringWebDriver`, you can do that by unregistering from that driver. The following API unregisters an event listener from a driver:

```
public EventFiringWebDriver unregister(WebDriverEventListener
eventListener)
```

The parameter of the method should be the event listener that wants to opt out of getting events notifications.

Summary

In this chapter, you have learned about `EventFiringWebDriver` and `EventListeners`, and how they work together to make the developer's life easy in order to debug what is going on at each step while the test cases get executed.

In the next chapter, we will learn how WebDriver handles I/O operations on a filesystem.

6
Dealing with I/O

In this chapter, we will see how to handle a filesystem using WebDriver in our test scripts. In our web application, there may be scenarios where we have to download files; this is something a test script developer has to deal with while writing test scripts. For this, you may have to work with the filesystem to copy files from one location to another, zip or unzip files, delete directories or files, and so on. Selenium WebDriver provides you a good set of classes to handle the filesystem. In this chapter, we will learn about the following three important classes of WebDriver:

- FileHandler
- TemporaryFileSystem
- Zip

Learning about the FileHandler class

In this section, we will look at different I/O actions that we can perform using WebDriver. We will basically go through all the methods that our FileHandler class offers us. To start with, let's look at the copy() methods. It has two overloaded methods.

Copying files from the source to the destination directory

WebDriver provides a method in the FileHandler class to copy the contents of the source directory to the destination directory. The API syntax for the method is as follows:

```
public static void copy(java.io.File from,
  java.io.File to) throws java.io.IOException
```

Using the preceding method, you can copy all the files of one directory to another. The example of the code for doing this is as follows; but, for it to work, you need to create two directories, `Src` and `Dest`, with two files `file1.rtf` and `file2.txt` in the `Src` directory, and some random text in those files:

```
public class CopyFromSrcToDestDir {
    public static void main(String... args){
        try {
            FileHandler.copy(new File("C:\\Src\\"), new File("C:\\
Dest\\"));
        } catch (IOException e) {
            e.printStackTrace();
        }
    }
}
```

The `copy()` method will copy all the files of `Src` directory to the `Dest` directory. You can also copy a specific file, say `file1.rtf`, by specifying its source and destination paths. So, the `copy()` method will look as follows:

```
FileHandler.copy(new File("C:\\Src\\file1.rtf"), new File("C:\\Dest\\
file1.rtf"));
```

If the entire path is not specified on the destination side, there will be an `IOException` thrown. The exception will look as follows:

```
java.io.FileNotFoundException: C:\Dest (Socket operation on non-socket)
    at java.io.FileOutputStream.open(Native Method)
    at java.io.FileOutputStream.<init>(Unknown Source)
    at java.io.FileOutputStream.<init>(Unknown Source)
    at org.openqa.selenium.io.FileHandler.copyFile(FileHandler.java:189)
    at org.openqa.selenium.io.FileHandler.copy(FileHandler.java:156)
    at org.openqa.selenium.io.FileHandler.copy(FileHandler.java:141)
    at com.packt.webdriver.chapter6.CopyFromSrcToDestDir.main(CopyFromSrcToDestDir.java:12)
```

Copying files from the source to the destination directory based on filename suffix

There is a overloaded method of the preceding `copy()` method that will copy all the files from the source directory to the destination directory with the same suffix. The API syntax for it is as follows:

```
public static void copy(java.io.File source,
java.io.File dest,java.lang.String suffix)
throws java.io.IOException
```

The third parameter shown in the following code is the suffix .txt, which is to be copied from the source directory to the destination directory. Before we see the code example, in the source directory, create file1.txt, file2.txt, file1.rtf and file2.rtf. Now, try to execute the following code, and see what happens:

```
public class CopySimilarFilesFromSrcToDestDir {
    public static void main(String... args){
        try {
            FileHandler.copy(new File("C:\\Src\\"), new
File("C:\\Dest\\"), ".txt");
        } catch (IOException e) {
            e.printStackTrace();
        }
    }
}
```

The preceding method will copy all the .txt files from the source directory to the destination directory. All the .rtf files will be left behind. Now create a file11.txt file in the source directory. Then modify the preceding code as shown in the following line:

```
FileHandler.copy(new File("C:\\Src\\"), new File("C:\\Dest\\"),
"1.txt");
```

Change the suffix to 1.txt instead of .txt. Delete all the files from the destination directory and execute the code. This should copy the file1.txt and file11.txt files to the destination directory.

Creating a directory

You can create a directory at any specified location with the specified name using the following method. The API syntax for this is as follows:

```
public static boolean createDir(java.io.File dir)
throws java.io.IOException
```

As the input parameter, you need to pass the full path of the directory that you want to create. The code example for using this method is as follows:

```
public class CreateDirectory {
    public static void main(String... args){
        try {
            FileHandler.createDir(new File("C:\\SelDir"));
        } catch (IOException e) {
            e.printStackTrace();
```

```
        }
      }
   }
```

The preceding code will create a directory named SelDir under the C:\\ directory.

Deleting a file or directory

The following method is used to delete a file or directory from the filesystem. The API syntax for the method is as follows:

```
public static boolean delete(java.io.File toDelete)
```

The input parameter can be a path to a file or directory. The FileHandler class will delete whatever is passed to it. The code example to delete the SelDir directory that was created in the previous section is as follows:

```
public class DeleteFileOrDirectory {
    public static void main(String... args){
        FileHandler.delete(new File("C:\\SelDir\\"));
    }
}
```

Understanding the IsZipped() method

The following method is used to verify whether or not a file is a ZIP file or not. This method of the FileHandler class will return a boolean value that is true if the file is a ZIP file; otherwise, it is false. The API syntax for it is as follows:

```
public static boolean isZipped(java.lang.String fileName)
```

The input parameter for the method is the name of the file that has to be verified. Now lets zip the Dest folder and verify it with the isZipped() method. The code is as follows:

```
public class IsZipped {
    public static void main(String... args){
        System.out.println(FileHandler.isZipped("C:\\Dest.zip"));
    }
}
```

The preceding code will print true, because it is a ZIP file. Now, if you modify the parameter filename as follows, the method will return false, because this is a folder and not a ZIP file:

```
FileHandler.isZipped("C:\\Dest")
```

Understanding the makeExecutable() method

Using the following method in the `FileHandler` class, you can set the permissions on a file to executable. If you are using Linux, it's like setting chmod 544 on your file. The API syntax for the method is as follows:

```
public static boolean makeExecutable(java.io.File file)
throws java.io.IOException
```

The input parameter is the file that has to be made executable. The code for it is as follows:

```
public class MakeExecutable {
    public static void main(String... args){
        try {
            FileHandler.makeExecutable(new File("C:\\Src\\file1.
txt"));
        } catch (IOException e) {
            e.printStackTrace();
        }
    }
}
```

In Linux and other *nix systems, the permissions on the file before and after executing the preceding code are shown in the following screenshot:

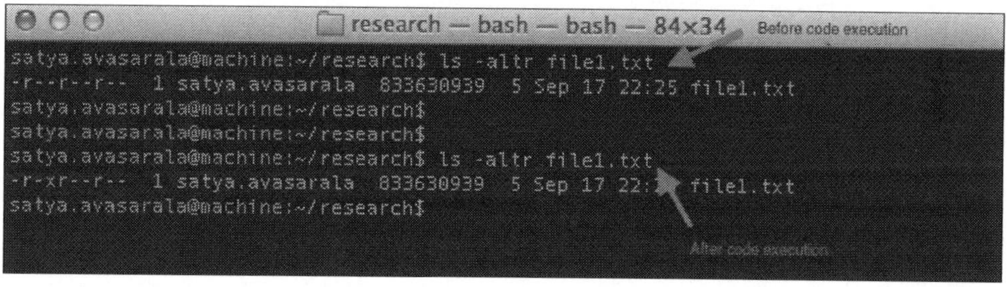

In Windows, you can right-click on the file to see the permissions in its **Properties | Security** window.

Understanding the makeWritable() method

Similar to the `makeExecutable()` method, we have a method in the `FileHandler` class that can alter the permissions for a file to make it writable. The API syntax for the method is as follows:

```
public static boolean makeWritable(java.io.File file)
throws java.io.IOException
```

This method also takes the file as an input parameter. The code example for it is as follows:

```
public class MakeWritable {
    public static void main(String... args){
        try {
            FileHandler.makeWritable(new
File("C:\\Src\\file1.txt"));
        } catch (IOException e) {
            e.printStackTrace();
        }
    }
}
```

The following screenshot shows the permissions on the file before and after executing the preceding code:

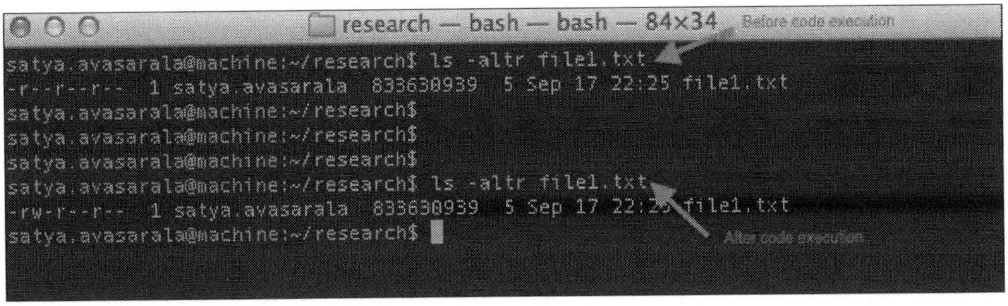

In Windows, you can right-click on the file to see the permissions in its **Properties | Security** window.

Reading a file

The `FileHandler` class also provides a method that can read the content of a file as a `String` variable. All the content of the target file is now available as a `String` variable in your test script. The API syntax for the method is as follows:

```
public static java.lang.String readAsString(java.io.File toRead)
throws java.io.IOException
```

The input parameter is the file path, the content of which has to be read. The code example for it is as follows:

```
public class ReadFileAsString {
    public static void main(String... args){
        try {
```

```
        String fileContent = FileHandler.readAsString(new
File("C:\\Src\\file1.txt"));
            System.out.println(fileContent);
        } catch (IOException e) {
            e.printStackTrace();
        }
    }
}
```

The preceding code should print all the contents of the file to the console. Make sure that there is some content in the file before you execute this code, just to make sure you see some content in the console.

Understanding the canExecute() method

The `FileHandler` class provides us another method that can verify whether or not a file is executable. This will validate the permissions on the file before giving us the result. If `executable` permissions were set on the file, this method will return `true`; otherwise, it returns `false`. The API syntax is as follows:

```
public static java.lang.Boolean canExecute(java.io.File file)
```

The input parameter is the file path that we are interested in determining whether or not it is executable. The return type is a `Boolean` value letting us know whether or not we can execute that file. The code example is as follows:

```
public class CanExecute {
    public static void main(String... args){
        try {
            System.out.println(FileHandler.canExecute(new File("C:\\
Src\\file1.txt")));
            FileHandler.makeExecutable(new File("C:\\Src\\file1.
txt"));
            System.out.println(FileHandler.canExecute(new File("C:\\
Src\\file1.txt")));
        } catch (IOException e) {
            e.printStackTrace();
        }
    }
}
```

Assuming, initially, that the permission for the `file1.txt` file is 444, which is ready-only, after executing the preceding code, you will see the output shown in the following screenshot:

The output states that initially you cannot execute the file, and after executing the `makeExecutable()` method on the file, the `canExecute()` method returns `true`.

Learning about the TemporaryFilesystem class

In this section, we will see the temporary filesystem that WebDriver uses. As the name suggests, the files that are created under temporary filesystem are temporary; that is, the files are deleted as soon as your test script is executed.

Understanding the default temporary filesystem

WebDriver generally uses your `AppData\Local\Temp` folder as your temporary filesystem on Windows. But we can figure that out. There is a method in the `TemporaryFilesystem` class that will show the default temporary filesystem that is being used by WebDriver. The API syntax for that method is as follows:

```
public static TemporaryFilesystem getDefaultTmpFS()
```

The preceding method will return the `TemporaryFilesystem` class based on the default temporary directory. The `TemporaryFilesystem` class doesn't have a direct method to print the absolute path of the temporary directory. To get that, lets create a directory in the temporary filesystem.

Creating a directory in DefaultTmpFS

To create a directory, the `TemporaryFilesystem` class has an built-in method. The API syntax for that is as follows:

```
public java.io.File createTempDir(java.lang.String prefix,
java.lang.String suffix)
```

The input parameters for the preceding method are the `prefix` and `suffix` strings for the directory you want to create. WebDriver will add the `prefix` and `suffix` strings to either ends of the random and unique name it generates for your directory in the temporary filesystem. Make sure you pass such `prefix` and `suffix` strings that will enable you to identify your directory. The return type is the file object representing your newly created directory.

The code that will create a directory in the default temporary filesystem is as follows:

```
public class DefaultTemporaryFileSystem {
    public static void main(String... args) {
        File f = TemporaryFilesystem.getDefaultTmpFS()
                .createTempDir("prefix", "suffix");
        System.out.println(f.getAbsolutePath());
        try {
            Thread.sleep(30000);
        } catch (InterruptedException e) {
            e.printStackTrace();
        }
    }
}
```

In the highlighted code, we got the default filesystem and created a directory there. The output of the execution is shown as follows:

In the output, `C:\Users\SATYAA~1\AppData\Local\Temp` represents the default filesystem location and `prefix3951927706786433878suffix` is the directory that we have just created. As discussed earlier, this directory gets deleted once the test script execution is over. In the preceding code, I have added a 30-second delay using the `Thread.sleep()` method so that we can open the temporary filesystem and see the newly created directory. Observe that the directory gets deleted once the test script execution is over.

Deleting a temporary directory

Although the `createTempDir()` method creates a temporary directory, the `deleteTempDir()` method deletes that temporary directory. The API syntax for the method is as follows:

```
public void deleteTempDir(java.io.File file)
```

The input parameter for this method is the directory file object that we have created. The code that uses this method is as follows:

```
public class DeleteTempDir {
    public static void main(String... args) {
        File f = TemporaryFilesystem.getDefaultTmpFS()
                .createTempDir("prefix", "suffix");
        System.out.println(f.getAbsolutePath());
        try {
            Thread.sleep(30000);
        } catch (InterruptedException e) {
            e.printStackTrace();
        }
        TemporaryFilesystem.getDefaultTmpFS().deleteTempDir(f);
        try {
            Thread.sleep(30000);
        } catch (InterruptedException e) {
            e.printStackTrace();
        }
    }
}
```

The highlighted code uses the `deleteTempDir()` method to delete the directory that we have created. The `Thread.sleep()` method is used to make sure you get time to see the directory while the execution is taking place.

Deleting multiple files

In the previous section, we have seen how to delete one temporary directory. But if we want to delete all the temporary directories we have created, there is a method to do that. The API syntax for that is as follows:

```
public void deleteTemporaryFiles()
```

The preceding method will delete all the temporary directories and files that we have created in the temporary filesystem. The code example to do that is as follows:

```
public class DeleteTemporaryFiles {
    public static void main(String... args) {
        File f1 = TemporaryFilesystem.getDefaultTmpFS()
                .createTempDir("prefix1", "suffix1");
        System.out.println("File1: "+f1.getAbsolutePath());
        File f2 = TemporaryFilesystem.getDefaultTmpFS()
                .createTempDir("prefix2", "suffix2");
        System.out.println("File1: "+f2.getAbsolutePath());
        try {
            Thread.sleep(30000);
        } catch (InterruptedException e) {
            e.printStackTrace();
        }
    TemporaryFilesystem.getDefaultTmpFS().deleteTemporaryFiles();
        try {
            Thread.sleep(30000);
        } catch (InterruptedException e) {
            e.printStackTrace();
        }
    }
}
```

In the previous code, we have created two directories, the names of which start with prefix1 and prefix2 and end with suffix1 and suffix2. Now, using the deleteTemporaryFiles() method, we have removed those two directories simultaneously.

Changing the temporary filesystem

Until now, we have created our temporary directories in the default temporary filesystem C:\Users\SATYAA~1\AppData\Local\Temp\. But, if we want to set another location as the temporary filesystem location for our test scripts, we can. The TemporaryFilesystem class provides a method for that. The API syntax for the method is as follows:

```
public static TemporaryFilesystem getTmpFsBasedOn(java.io.File
directory)
```

The input parameter for this method is the directory that we wish to make our temporary filesystem. Let's see the following code example showing how we can change our temporary filesystem:

```
public class ChangeTmpFS {
    public static void main(String... args) {
        TemporaryFilesystem tmpFS = TemporaryFilesystem.
getTmpFsBasedOn(new File("C:\\TmpFS"));
        File f = tmpFS.createTempDir("prefix1", "suffix1");
        System.out.println(f.getAbsolutePath());
        try {
            Thread.sleep(30000);
        } catch (InterruptedException e) {
            e.printStackTrace();
        }
    }
}
```

In the preceding code, we have chosen `C:\\TmpFS` as our temporary filesystem, and having done that, created a directory within it. The output of the preceding code will be the following:

```
C:\TmpFS\prefix11845956783678412581suffix1
```

Learning about the Zip class

WebDriver libraries also give test script developers the option of dealing with the ZIP files. They will let you zip a directory and also unzip a zipped file into a directory.

Compressing a directory

You can compress a directory into a ZIP file using the method provided by WebDriver. The API syntax for it is as follows:

```
public void zip(java.io.File inputDir,
java.io.File output)
throws java.io.IOException
```

The input parameters are the directory that has to be compressed and the output file to which the ZIP file should be written. The code to do that is as follows:

```
public class ZipDir {
    public static void main(String... args){
        Zip zip = new Zip();
        try {
            zip.zip(new File("C:\\TmpFS"), new File("C:\\TmpFS.zip"));
        } catch (IOException e) {
            e.printStackTrace();
        }
    }
}
```

Executing the preceding code will create a `TmpFS.zip` file with all the zipped contents of the `TmpFS` directory.

Decompressing a directory

Now, let's have a look at the reverse process. You can decompress or unzip the file created in the previous section. For this, the `Zip` class provides a method named `unzip`. The API syntax for that method is as follows:

```
public void unzip(java.io.File source,
java.io.File outputDir)
throws java.io.IOException
```

The input parameters are the ZIP file and the `output` directory. The code for it is demonstrated as follows:

```
public class UnzipToDir {
    public static void main(String... args){
        Zip zip = new Zip();
        try {
            zip.unzip(new File("C:\\TmpFS.zip"), new
File("C:\\"));
        } catch (IOException e) {
            e.printStackTrace();
        }
    }
}
```

Executing the preceding code will decompress the ZIP file to a folder using the same name.

Summary

We have seen various file-handling classes and methods of WebDriver that will help you, as a test script developer, have better control over the filesystem, and write better test cases in your automation.

In the next chapter, we will learn about executing test scripts on remote machines using RemoteWebDriver and supporting test scripts, which are coded for Selenium 1, with WebDriver.

7

Exploring RemoteWebDriver and WebDriverBackedSelenium

So far, we have created our test cases and tried to execute them on various browsers. All of these tests were executed against the browsers that were installed on a local machine where test cases reside. This may not be possible at all times. There is a high possibility that you may be working on Mac or Linux, but want to execute your tests on IE on a Windows machine. In this chapter, we will learn about the following topics:

- Executing test cases on a remote machine using `RemoteWebDriver`

- A detailed explanation of the JSON wire protocol

- A brief history about how Selenium 1 test cases were written, and how we can migrate them to use WebDriver APIs using the `WebDriverBackedSelenium` class

Introducing RemoteWebDriver

`RemoteWebDriver` is an implementation class of the `WebDriver` interface that a test script developer can use to execute their test scripts via the `RemoteWebDriver` server on a remote machine. There are two parts to `RemoteWebDriver`: a server and a client. Before we start working with them, let us rewind and see what we have been doing.

The following diagram explains what we have been doing so far.

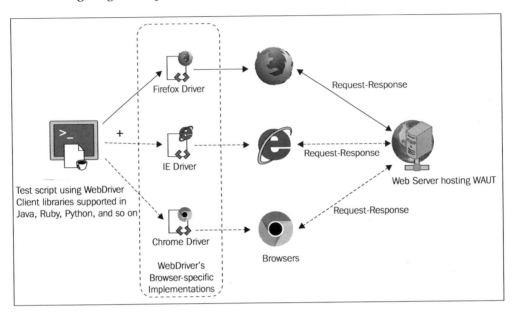

The test script using WebDriver client libraries, Firefox Driver (or IE Driver or Chrome Driver), and Firefox browser (or IE browser or Chrome browser) are sitting on the same machine. The browser is loading the web application, which may or may not be hosted remotely; anyway, this is not within the scope of our discussion.

We will discuss different scenarios of test script execution as follows:

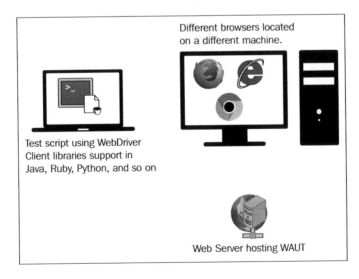

The test script is located on a local machine, while the browsers are installed on a remote machine. In this scenario, RemoteWebDriver comes into the picture. As mentioned earlier, there are two components associated with RemoteWebDriver: the server and the client. Let us start with the RemoteWebDriver server.

Understanding the RemoteWebDriver server

The RemoteWebDriver server is a component that listens on a port for various requests from a RemoteWebDriver client. Once it receives the requests, it forwards them to any of the following: Firefox Driver, IE Driver, or Chrome Driver, whichever is asked.

Downloading the server

Let us download the RemoteWebDriver server and start running it. You can download it from https://code.google.com/p/selenium/downloads/, but for our purposes, let us download a specific version of it as we are using WebDriver Version 2.33.0. The specific version can be downloaded from https://code.google.com/p/selenium/downloads/detail?name=selenium-server-standalone-2.33.0.jar.

This server JAR should be downloaded to the remote machine on which the browsers are located. Also, make sure the remote machine has Java runtime installed on it.

Running the server

Open your command-line tool on the remote machine and navigate to the location to which you have downloaded the JAR file. Now, to start the RemoteWebDriver server, execute the following command:

```
java -jar selenium-server-standalone-2.33.0.jar
```

The following screenshot shows what you should see in your console:

```
Command Prompt - java -jar selenium-server-standalone-2.33.0.jar

C:\>java -jar selenium-server-standalone-2.33.0.jar
Oct 05, 2013 2:40:55 PM org.openqa.grid.selenium.GridLauncher main
INFO: Launching a standalone server
14:41:47.994 INFO - Java: Oracle Corporation 23.21-b01
14:41:47.995 INFO - OS: Windows 8 6.2 x86
14:41:48.016 INFO - v2.33.0, with Core v2.33.0. Built from revision 4e90c97
14:41:48.687 INFO - RemoteWebDriver instances should connect to: http://127.0.0.
1:4444/wd/hub
14:41:48.688 INFO - Version Jetty/5.1.x
14:41:48.689 INFO - Started HttpContext[/selenium-server/driver,/selenium-server
/driver]
14:41:48.690 INFO - Started HttpContext[/selenium-server,/selenium-server]
14:41:48.690 INFO - Started HttpContext[/,/]
14:41:48.935 INFO - Started org.openqa.jetty.jetty.servlet.ServletHandler@123b9c
1
14:41:48.935 INFO - Started HttpContext[/wd,/wd]
14:41:48.958 INFO - Started SocketListener on 0.0.0.0:4444
14:41:48.959 INFO - Started org.openqa.jetty.jetty.Server@136bdda
```

Now, the server has started and is listening on the `<remote-machine-ip>:4444` address for remote connections from the `RemoteWebDriver` client. Now the previously seen image (the second image in the *Introducing RemoteWebDriver* section) will appear as follows:

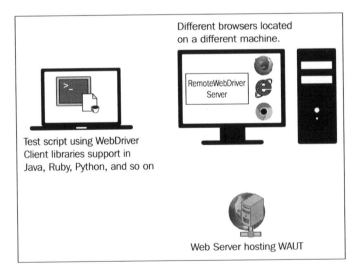

[142]

Understanding the RemoteWebDriver client

Now that we have our `RemoteWebDriver` server up and running, it is time for us to create the `RemoteWebDriver` client. Fortunately, we don't have to do anything much to create a `RemoteWebDriver` client. It's nothing but the language-binding client libraries that serve as a `RemoteWebDriver` client. The client, as it used to when executing tests locally, translates your test script requests to JSON payload and sends them across to the `RemoteWebDriver` server using the JSON wire protocol.

When you execute your tests locally, the WebDriver client libraries talk to your Firefox Driver, IE Driver, or Chrome Driver directly. Now, when you try to execute your tests remotely, the WebDriver client libraries talk to the `RemoteWebDriver` server and the server talks to either the Firefox Driver, IE Driver, or Chrome Driver, whichever the WebDriver client asks for.

Converting an existing test script to use RemoteWebDriver server

Let us take a test script that we have executed locally; that is, where the test scripts and the browser were on the same machine:

```
public class ExistingTest {
  public static void main(String... args){
    WebDriver driver = new FirefoxDriver();
  }
}
```

The preceding test script creates an instance of Firefox Driver and launches the Firefox browser. Now let us try to convert this test script to use the `RemoteWebDriver` server that we have started earlier. Before we do that, let us see the constructor of `RemoteWebDriver`, which is as follows:

```
RemoteWebDriver(java.net.URL remoteAddress,
Capabilities desiredCapabilities)
```

The input parameters for the constructor are one of the addresses of the `RemoteWebDriver` server running on the remote machine and the desired capabilities your test script needs. We will see those desired capabilities shortly.

Now, let's modify the test script to use `RemoteWebDriver`. Replace `WebDriver driver = new FirefoxDriver();` with the following code:

```
DesiredCapabilities capabilities = new DesiredCapabilities();
RemoteWebDriver remoteWD = null;
try {
```

```
    remoteWD = new RemoteWebDriver(new
URL("http://10.172.10.1:4444/wd/hub"),capabilities);
} catch (MalformedURLException e) {
        e.printStackTrace();
}
```

We have created a `RemoteWebDriver` instance that tries to connect to
`http://10.172.10.1:4444/wd/hub`, where the `RemoteWebDriver` server is
running and listening for requests. Having done that, we also need to specify
which browser your test case should get executed on. This can be done using the
`DesiredCapabilities` instance. So let's ask `RemoteWebDriver` to run our test scripts
on the Firefox browser. The preceding code will be changed to the following code:

```
DesiredCapabilities capabilities = new DesiredCapabilities();
capabilities.setBrowserName("firefox");
RemoteWebDriver remoteWD = null;
try {
    remoteWD = new RemoteWebDriver(new URL("http:// 10.172.10.1:4444/
wd/hub"),capabilities);
} catch (MalformedURLException e) {
        e.printStackTrace();
}
```

Now `RemoteWebDriver` will launch the Firefox browser and execute your test case
on it. So the modified test case will look as follows:

```
package com.packt.webdriver.chapter7;

import java.net.MalformedURLException;
import java.net.URL;
import org.openqa.selenium.remote.DesiredCapabilities;
import org.openqa.selenium.remote.RemoteWebDriver;

public class UsingRemoteWebDriver {
    public static void main(String... args){
        DesiredCapabilities capabilities = new DesiredCapabilities();
        capabilities.setBrowserName("firefox");
        RemoteWebDriver remoteWD = null;
        try {
            remoteWD = new RemoteWebDriver(new URL("http://
10.172.10.1:4444/wd/hub"),capabilities);
        } catch (MalformedURLException e) {
            e.printStackTrace();
        }
    }
}
```

Now execute this test script from your local machine to establish a connection between the `RemoteWebDriver` client and the `RemoteWebDriver` server. The `RemoteWebDriver` server will launch the Firefox browser. The following is the output you will see in the console where the `RemoteWebDriver` server is running:

```
15:57:11.761 INFO - Creating a new session for Capabilities [{browserName=firefox}]

15:58:06.338 INFO - Done: /session

15:58:06.352 INFO - Executing: org.openqa.selenium.remote.server.handler.GetSess

ionCapabilities@1ccbdbe at URL: /session/b248d41f-fc5c-4010-bac1-8862cbb3372f)

15:58:06.352 INFO - Done: /session/b248d41f-fc5c-4010-bac1-8862cbb3372f
```

It says that a new session with the desired capabilities is being created, which, after being created, prints the session ID on to the console. At any point in time, you can view all of the sessions that are established with the `RemoteWebDriver` server by navigating to `http://10.172.10.1:4444/wd/hub`.

It will give the entire list of sessions that the `RemoteWebDriver` server is currently handling. The screenshot of this is as follows:

This is a very basic portal that lets the test script developer see all of the sessions created with the `RemoteWebDriver` server and perform some basic operations on it, such as terminating a session, taking a screenshot of a session, loading a script to a session, and seeing all of the desired capabilities of a session. The following screenshot shows all of the default desired capabilities of our current session.

You can see the popup by hovering over the **Capabilities** link, as shown in the following screenshot:

Those are the default desired capabilities that are set implicitly by the server for this session. Now, we have successfully established a connection between our test script, which is using a RemoteWebDriver client on one machine, and the RemoteWebDriver server on another machine. The original diagram of running the test scripts remotely is as follows:

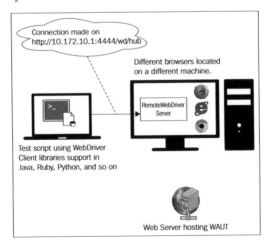

Using RemoteWebDriver for the Firefox browser

We have seen how the `RemoteWebDriver` client is connected to the `RemoteWebDriver` server. Now we will see what actions the `RemoteWebDriver` server performs to load your application, which is being tested on the Firefox browser.

As soon as the server receives a request on port `4444`, it verifies which browser has asked for the desired capabilities. When the server figures out that the request is for the Firefox browser, it launches the Firefox Driver as an extension to the Firefox browser, as discussed in *Chapter 4, Different Available WebDrivers*.

The `RemoteWebDriver` server opens a socket connection, usually to the Firefox Driver, on port `7055`. From then on, all of your test script commands are handed over by the `RemoteWebDriver` server to Firefox Driver through this socket. So, from where did the `RemoteWebDriver` server find the Firefox Driver? Firefox Driver comes along with the `RemoteWebDriver` server JAR file. You don't have to download or start it explicitly, unlike with IE Driver or Chrome Driver.

Using `DesiredCapabilities`, you can specify the `RemoteWebDriver` server on which you want your test script commands to be executed on Firefox browser, as shown in the following code:

```
DesiredCapabilities capabilities = new DesiredCapabilities();
capabilities.setBrowserName("firefox");
```

The parameter passed to the `setBrowserName()` method will indicate which browser to launch. In this case, it is `"firefox"`. The parameters that can be passed to this method are `chrome`, `htmlunit`, `internet explorer`, and so on; they are case-sensitive. Now, let us modify our test case to pass some commands to the browser, as shown in the following code:

```
public class UsingRemoteWebDriver {
    public static void main(String... args){
        DesiredCapabilities capabilities = new DesiredCapabilities();
        capabilities.setBrowserName("firefox");
        RemoteWebDriver remoteWD = null;
        try {
            remoteWD = new RemoteWebDriver(new
URL("http://10.172.10.1:4444/wd/hub"),capabilities);
        } catch (MalformedURLException e) {
            e.printStackTrace();
        }
        remoteWD.get("http://www.google.com");
```

```
        remoteWD.findElement(By.name("q")).sendKeys("Packt Publishing");
    }
}
```

As seen in a previous section, a session is established between the `RemoteWebDriver` client and the server. After that, the commands are interpreted by the `RemoteWebDriver` server and passed on to the Firefox Driver that is running on `http://localhost:7055`. The following screenshot shows the commands interpreted by the server and the output seen in the console on which the `RemoteWebDriver` server is running:

On the console, we see three different commands being interpreted, which were sent from the test script or the `RemoteWebDriver` client to the server.

The first command from the test script is as follows:

```
remoteWD.get("http://www.google.com");
```

Its corresponding execution on the server side is as follows:

19:05:48.477 INFO - Executing: [get: http://www.google.com] at URL: /session/5feaf137-0a95-4370-a6fa-bc9cf417b030/url)

The second command from the test script is as follows:

```
WebElement element = remoteWD.findElement(By.name("q"));
```

Its corresponding execution on the server side is as follows:

19:05:52.371 INFO - Executing: [find element: By.name: q] at URL: /session/5feaf137-0a95-4370-a6fa-bc9cf417b030/element)

The third command from the test script is as follows:

```
element.sendKeys("Packt Publishing");
```

Its corresponding execution on the server side is as follows:

```
19:05:52.657 INFO - Executing: [send keys: 0 org.openqa.selenium.support.
events.EventFiringWebDriver$EventFiringWebElement@7f150a63, [Packt
Publishing]] at URL: /session/5feaf137-0a95-4370-a6fa-bc9cf417b030/
element/0/value)
```

Now, our initial diagram of the process of running test scripts looks as follows:

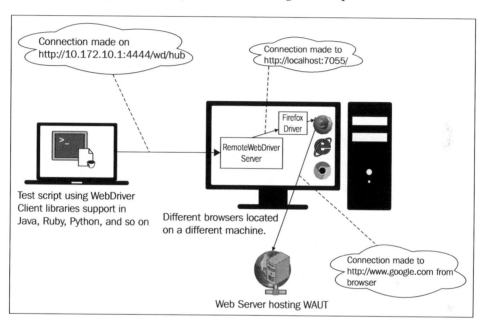

Using RemoteWebDriver and the IE browser

Using IE browser to execute our test scripts is similar to using the Firefox browser, except for a couple of variations in how IE Driver is launched. Let's see this by changing the test script that we used for the Firefox browser to the following script, using "internet explorer":

```java
public class UsingRemoteWebDriverAndIEBrowser {
    public static void main(String... args){
        DesiredCapabilities capabilities
                    = new DesiredCapabilities();
        capabilities.setBrowserName("internet explorer");
        RemoteWebDriver remoteWD = null;
        try {
            remoteWD = new RemoteWebDriver(new
URL("http://10.172.10.1:4444/wd/hub"),capabilities);
```

```
        } catch (MalformedURLException e) {
           e.printStackTrace();
        }
        remoteWD.get("http://www.google.com");
        WebElement element = remoteWD.findElement(By.name("q"));
        element.sendKeys("Packt Publishing");
    }
}
```

We are passing `"internet explorer"` to the `setBrowserName()` method. Now, if you try to execute this code, you will see the following exception:

```
Exception in thread "main" org.openqa.selenium.WebDriverException: The path
to the driver executable must be set by the webdriver.ie.driver system property;
for more information, see http://code.google.com/p/selenium/wiki/
InternetExplorerDriver. The latest version can be downloaded from http://
code.google.com/p/selenium/downloads/list
```

The exception says that we have set the path for the IE Driver executable. This is a little different from Firefox Driver, because the `RemoteWebDriver` server has the Firefox Driver bundle within it's JAR and can thus launch it whenever required. But, for IE Driver, you need to specify the path for the executable explicitly. Stopping the `RemoteWebDriver` server and restarting it using the following command will do this:

```
C:\>java -Dwebdriver.ie.driver="C:\IEDriverServer.exe" -jar selenium-
server-standalone-2.33.0.jar
```

Now the `RemoteWebDriver` server knows the location of your IE Driver and will launch it whenever there is a request for the IE browser from the `RemoteWebDriver` client. Try executing the preceding test script now, and you should see the IE browser getting launched and executing your test commands. The output on the console of the `RemoteWebDriver` server will appear as follows:

```
10:32:20.808 INFO - Executing: [new session: {browserName=internet
explorer}] at URL: /session)
10:32:20.811 INFO - Creating a new session for Capabilities
[{browserName=internet explorer}]
Started InternetExplorerDriver server (32-bit)
2.35.3.0
Listening on port 3382
```

```
10:32:23.377 INFO - Done: /session

10:32:23.392 INFO - Executing: org.openqa.selenium.remote.server.handler.
GetSessionCapabilities@37783b at URL: /se

ssion/357fd3ed-3165-4284-a165-7af59f8034b6)

10:32:23.395 INFO - Done: /session/357fd3ed-3165-4284-a165-7af59f8034b6

10:32:23.419 INFO - Executing: [get: http://www.google.com] at URL: /
session/357fd3ed-3165-4284-a165-7af59f8034b6/

url)

10:32:25.071 INFO - Done: /session/357fd3ed-3165-4284-a165-7af59f8034b6/
url

10:32:25.083 INFO - Executing: [find element: By.name: q] at URL: /
session/357fd3ed-3165-4284-a165-7af59f8034b6/element)

10:32:25.122 INFO - Done: /session/357fd3ed-3165-4284-a165-7af59f8034b6/
element

10:32:25.136 INFO - Executing: [send keys: 0 org.openqa.selenium.support.
events.EventFiringWebDriver$EventFiringWe

bElement@57f37f37, [Packt Publishing]] at URL: /session/357fd3ed-3165-
4284-a165-7af59f8034b6/element/0/value)

10:32:25.625 INFO - Done: /session/357fd3ed-3165-4284-a165-7af59f8034b6/
element/0/value
```

So, the `RemoteWebDriver` server has started the IE Driver, created a connection with it, and started executing the three test script commands. The remote test script execution scenario looks as follows:

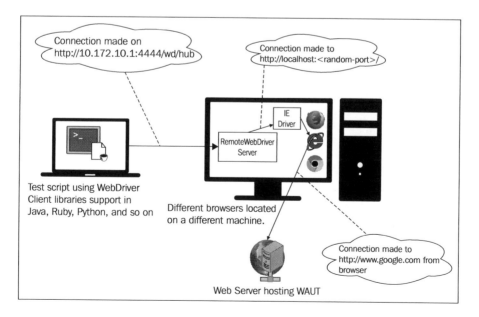

Using RemoteWebDriver and the Chrome browser

Using RemoteWebDriver with the Chrome browser is exactly the same as the IE browser. The browser name should be set to `"chrome"` for the `setBrowserName()` method and the `RemoteWebDriver` server should be started with the following command:

```
C:\>java -Dwebdriver.ie.driver="C:\IEDriverServer.exe"
       -Dwebdriver.chrome.driver="C:\chromedriver.exe"
       -jar selenium-server-standalone-2.33.0.jar
```

Now, this `RemoteWebDriver` server is ready to accept requests from `RemoteWebDriver` clients for both IE and Chrome browsers.

The test script for the Chrome browser will appear as follows:

```java
public class UsingRemoteWebDriverAndChromeBrowser {
    public static void main(String... args){
        DesiredCapabilities capabilities
                = new DesiredCapabilities();
        capabilities.setBrowserName("chrome");

        RemoteWebDriver remoteWD = null;
        try {
            remoteWD = new RemoteWebDriver(new
URL("http://10.172.10.1:4444/wd/hub"),capabilities);

        } catch (MalformedURLException e) {
            e.printStackTrace();
        }
        remoteWD.get("http://www.google.com");
        WebElement element = remoteWD.findElement(By.name("q"));
        element.sendKeys("Packt Publishing");
    }
}
```

The console output for the `RemoteWebDriver` server, after executing the preceding test script, is as follows:

```
12:54:59.407 INFO - Executing: [new session: {browserName=chrome}] at
URL: /session)

12:54:59.517 INFO - Creating a new session for Capabilities
[{browserName=chrome}]

Starting ChromeDriver (v2.2) on port 24483
```

```
12:55:01.544 INFO - Done: /session
12:55:01.558 INFO - Executing: org.openqa.selenium.remote.server.handler.
GetSessionCapabilities@683e68 at URL: /se
ssion/bfd0c71d-e326-4286-9f92-fa3046a1ccb7)
12:55:01.562 INFO - Done: /session/bfd0c71d-e326-4286-9f92-fa3046a1ccb7
12:55:01.586 INFO - Executing: [get: http://www.google.com] at URL: /
session/bfd0c71d-e326-4286-9f92-fa3046a1ccb7/
url)
12:55:04.655 INFO - Done: /session/bfd0c71d-e326-4286-9f92-fa3046a1ccb7/
url
12:55:04.669 INFO - Executing: [find element: By.name: q] at URL: /
session/bfd0c71d-e326-4286-9f92-fa3046a1ccb7/element)
12:55:04.799 INFO - Done: /session/bfd0c71d-e326-4286-9f92-fa3046a1ccb7/
element
12:55:04.816 INFO - Executing: [send keys: 0 org.openqa.selenium.support.
events.EventFiringWebDriver$EventFiringWe
bElement@4f4b7de3, [Packt Publishing]] at URL: /session/bfd0c71d-e326-
4286-9f92-fa3046a1ccb7/element/0/value)
12:55:05.361 INFO - Done: /session/bfd0c71d-e326-4286-9f92-fa3046a1ccb7/
element/0/value
```

The `RemoteWebDriver` server has started the Chrome Driver on port `24483` and executed the test script commands on the Chrome browser. The remote test script execution scenario in this case looks as shown in the following diagram:

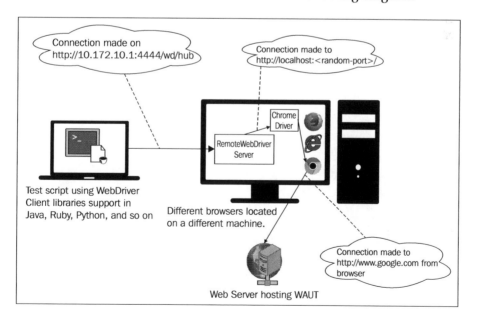

Extending the RemoteWebDriver client to take screenshots

If you compare the signatures of RemoteWebDriver to those of Firefox Driver, IE Driver, or Chrome Driver, you will observe that all of the other drivers implement the TakesScreenshot interface. This will allow the instances of those drivers to take a screenshot of your page, which is loaded on the browsers. But, if you try to do the same thing using the instance of a RemoteWebDriver, your test script will fail, throwing a ClassCastException.

The following is the code you can try:

```
public class ScreenShotUsingRemoteWebDriver {
    public static void main(String... args){
        DesiredCapabilities capabilities
                    = new DesiredCapabilities();
        capabilities.setBrowserName("firefox");
        WebDriver remoteWD = null;
        try {
            remoteWD = new RemoteWebDriver(new
URL("http://10.172.10.1:4444/wd/hub"),capabilities);
        } catch (MalformedURLException e) {
            e.printStackTrace();
        }
        remoteWD.get("http://www.google.com");
        WebElement element = remoteWD.findElement(By.name("q"));
        element.sendKeys("Packt Publishing");

        File scrFile = ((TakesScreenshot)remoteWD).
getScreenshotAs(OutputType.FILE);
        System.out.println(scrFile.getAbsolutePath());
    }
}
```

The test script will fail with the following exception:

```
Exception in thread "main" java.lang.ClassCastException:
org.openqa.selenium.remote.RemoteWebDriver cannot be cast to
org.openqa.selenium.TakesScreenshot
    at
com.packt.webdriver.chapter7.ScreenShotUsingRemoteWebDriver.main(Screen
ShotUsingRemoteWebDriver.java:33)
```

This is because `RemoteWebDriver` doesn't implement the `TakesScreenshot` interface. There are the following two ways to deal with this:

- The first approach is to create your own `WebDriver` class that extends the `RemoteWebDriver` class and implements the `TakesScreenshot` interface by providing the implementation for the `getScreenshotAs()` method, as shown in the following code:

```
public class CustomRemoteWebDriver extends RemoteWebDriver
implements TakesScreenshot {
    public <X> X getScreenshotAs(OutputType<X> target) {
        // Get the screenshot as base64.
        String base64 = execute(DriverCommand.SCREENSHOT).
getValue().toString();
        // ... and convert it.
        return target.convertFromBase64Png(base64);
    }
}
```

  Instantiate the `CustomRemoteWebDriver` class instead of directly instantiating `RemoteWebDriver` in your class, which will allow you to take the screenshot.

- The second approach is to use the `Augmenter` class. This will enhance the `RemoteWebDriver` instance based on the set `DesiredCapabilities`. This is still in its early stages of implementation, so using it may result in unexpected results sometimes. Using this, you can take the screenshots. Our test script, after using the `Augmenter` class, will look as follows:

```
public class ScreenShotUsingRemoteWebDriver {
    public static void main(String... args) {
        DesiredCapabilities capabilities = new
DesiredCapabilities();
        capabilities.setBrowserName("firefox");
        WebDriver remoteWD = null;
        try {
            remoteWD = new RemoteWebDriver(new
URL("http://10.172.10.1:4444/wd/hub"),capabilities);
        } catch (MalformedURLException e) {
            e.printStackTrace();
        }
        remoteWD.get("http://www.google.com");
        WebElement element = remoteWD.findElement(By.name("q"));
        element.sendKeys("Packt Publishing");
```

```
        remoteWD = new Augmenter().augment(remoteWD);
        File scrFile = ((TakesScreenshot)remoteWD).
getScreenshotAs(OutputType.FILE);
            System.out.println(scrFile.getAbsolutePath());
    }
}
```

Thus, using the `RemoteWebDriver` class, you will still be able to take screenshots of the web pages loaded on your browsers.

Understanding the JSON wire protocol

All this while, in many places, we have mentioned that WebDriver uses the JSON wire protocol to communicate between client libraries and different drivers (that is, Firefox Driver, IE Driver, Chrome Driver, and so on) implementations. In this section, we will see exactly what it is and which different JSON APIs a client library should implement to talk to the drivers.

JavaScript Object Notation (JSON) is used to represent objects with complex data structures. It is used primarily to transfer data between a server and a client on the web. It has very much become an industry standard for various REST web services, playing a strong alternative to XML.

A sample JSON file, saved as a `.json` file, will look as follows:

```
{
    "firstname": "John",
    "lastname": "Doe",
    "address": {
        "streetnumber":"678",
        "street":"Victoria Street",
        "city":"Richmond",
        "state":"Victoria",
        "country":"Australia"
    }
    "phone":"+61470315430"
}
```

A client can send a person's details to a server in the preceding JSON format, which the server can parse and create an instance of the `Person` object for use in its execution. Later, the response can be sent back by the server to the client in the JSON format, the data of which the client can use to create an object of a class. This process of converting an object's data to the JSON format and JSON-formatted data to an object is named **serialization** and **de-serialization**, respectively, which is quite common in REST web services these days.

Our WebDriver uses the same approach to communicate between client libraries (language bindings) and drivers, such as Firefox Driver, IE Driver, Chrome Driver, and so on. Similarly, the `RemoteWebDriver` client and the `RemoteWebDriver` server use the JSON wire protocol to communicate among themselves. But, all of these drivers use it under the hood, hiding all of the implementation details from us and making our lives simpler. For any existing or new client library, they should provide implementations for building all of the WebDriver JSON APIs, and any existing or new WebDriver should handle these requests and provide implementations for them. The list of APIs for various actions that we can take on a webpage is as follows:

```
/status
/session
/sessions
/session/:sessionId
/session/:sessionId/timeouts
/session/:sessionId/timeouts/async_script
/session/:sessionId/timeouts/implicit_wait
/session/:sessionId/window_handle
/session/:sessionId/window_handles
/session/:sessionId/url
/session/:sessionId/forward
/session/:sessionId/back
/session/:sessionId/refresh
/session/:sessionId/execute
/session/:sessionId/execute_async
/session/:sessionId/screenshot
/session/:sessionId/ime/available_engines
/session/:sessionId/ime/active_engine
.  .  .

.  .  .
/session/:sessionId/touch/flick
/session/:sessionId/touch/flick
/session/:sessionId/location
/session/:sessionId/local_storage
/session/:sessionId/local_storage/key/:key
/session/:sessionId/local_storage/size
/session/:sessionId/session_storage
/session/:sessionId/session_storage/key/:key
/session/:sessionId/session_storage/size
/session/:sessionId/log
/session/:sessionId/log/types
/session/:sessionId/application_cache/status
```

The complete documentation is available at `https://code.google.com/p/` `selenium/wiki/JsonWireProtocol`.

The client libraries will translate your test script commands to the JSON format and send the requests to the appropriate WebDriver API. The WebDriver will parse these requests and take necessary actions on the web page.

Let us see that with an example. Suppose your test script has a the following code:

```
driver.get("http://www.google.com");
```

The client library will translate that to JSON by building a JSON payload and post the request to the appropriate API. In this case, the API that handles the `driver.` `get(URL)` method is as follows:

```
/session/:sessionId/url
```

The following code shows what happens in the client library layer before the request is sent to the driver; the request is sent to the `RemoteWebDriver` server running on `10.172.10.1:4444`:

```
HttpClient httpClient = new DefaultHttpClient();
HttpPost postMethod  = new HttpPost("http://10.172.10.1:4444/wd/hub/
session/"+sessionId+"/url");
JSONObject jo=new JSONObject();
jo.put("url","http://www.google.com");
StringEntity input = new StringEntity(jo.toString());
input.setContentEncoding("UTF-8");
input.setContentEncoding(new BasicHeader(HTTP.CONTENT_TYPE,
"application/json"));
postMethod.setEntity(input);
HttpResponse response = httpClient.execute(postMethod);
```

The `RemoteWebDriver` server will forward that request to the driver; the driver will execute the test script commands that arrive in the preceding format on the web application under the test that is loaded in the browser.

The following diagram shows what data flows at each stage:

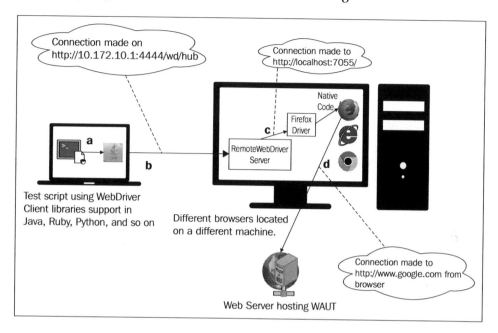

The following table shows which command is executed at each stage:

Stage in the preceding diagram	Command executed at that stage
a	`driver.get("http://www.google.com");`

b	`"http://10.172.10.1:4444/wd/hub/`
	`session/"+sessionId+"/url"`
	`{`
	`"url": "http://www.google.com"`
	`}`

c	`"http://localhost:7705/`
	`{`
	`"url": "http://www.google.com"`
	`}`

Native Code	Talks natively to the browser
d	`"http://www.google.com"`

In the previous diagram, the first stage is communication between your test script and client library. The data or command that flows between them is represented as **a** in the image; **a** is nothing but the following code:

```
driver.get("http://www.google.com");
```

The client library, as soon as it receives the preceding command, will convert it to the JSON format and communicate with the `RemoteWebDriver` server, which is represented as **b**.

Next, the `RemoteWebDriver` server forwards the JSON payload request to the Firefox Driver (in this case), and the data that flows through is represented as **c**.

Firefox Driver will speak to the Firefox browser natively, and then the browser will send a request for the asked URL to load, which is represented as **d**.

Replacing the client library with your own code

Replacing the client library with your own code is probably is not the best idea to replace the client libraries with your code in real-time testing, because they handle all of the serialization and de-serialization while letting you concentrate on writing the test scripts for your application. But, let's do that to get a more clear understanding of what exactly our client libraries do and how they communicate with the drivers on the JSON wire protocol.

To do this, you need to download some JAR files, as shown in the following steps:

1. The first one is the **Apache HttpClient** and the **Apache Wink**. The Apache HttpClient is used to send requests from a client to the server over HTTP. Apache Wink is used to create JSON-formatted objects. You can download Apache HttpClient 4.3 from `http://hc.apache.org/downloads.cgi`. Download the ZIP file and add the JAR files under the `lib` folder to your project in Eclipse. You can download Apache Wink 1.4 from `http://wink.apache.org/downloads.html`. Download the ZIP file and add the JAR files from the `lib` and `dist` folders.

2. After adding the JAR files, your Java build path in Eclipse should look
   as follows:

```
JARs and class folders on the build path:
  ▶ 🗔 activation-1.1.jar - /Users/satya.avasarala/Downloads/apache-wink-1.4/lib
  ▶ 🗔 commons-codec-1.6.jar - /Users/satya.avasarala/Downloads/httpcomponents-client-4.3-bin (1
  ▶ 🗔 commons-lang-2.3.jar - /Users/satya.avasarala/Downloads/apache-wink-1.4/lib
  ▶ 🗔 commons-logging-1.1.3.jar - /Users/satya.avasarala/Downloads/httpcomponents-client-4.3-bi
  ▶ 🗔 fluent-hc-4.3.jar - /Users/satya.avasarala/Downloads/httpcomponents-client-4.3-bin (1)/lib
  ▶ 🗔 geronimo-jaxrs_1.1_spec-1.0.jar - /Users/satya.avasarala/Downloads/apache-wink-1.4/lib
  ▶ 🗔 httpclient-4.3.jar - /Users/satya.avasarala/Downloads/httpcomponents-client-4.3-bin (1)/lib
  ▶ 🗔 httpclient-cache-4.3.jar - /Users/satya.avasarala/Downloads/httpcomponents-client-4.3-bin (1
  ▶ 🗔 httpcore-4.3.jar - /Users/satya.avasarala/Downloads/httpcomponents-client-4.3-bin (1)/lib
  ▶ 🗔 httpmime-4.3.jar - /Users/satya.avasarala/Downloads/httpcomponents-client-4.3-bin (1)/lib
  ▶ 🗔 jaxb-api-2.2.jar - /Users/satya.avasarala/Downloads/apache-wink-1.4/lib
  ▶ 🗔 jaxb-impl-2.2.1.1.jar - /Users/satya.avasarala/Downloads/apache-wink-1.4/lib
  ▶ 🗔 slf4j-api-1.6.1.jar - /Users/satya.avasarala/Downloads/apache-wink-1.4/lib
  ▶ 🗔 slf4j-simple-1.6.1.jar - /Users/satya.avasarala/Downloads/apache-wink-1.4/lib
  ▶ 🗔 stax-api-1.0-2.jar - /Users/satya.avasarala/Downloads/apache-wink-1.4/lib
  ▶ 🗔 wink-1.4.jar - /Users/satya.avasarala/Downloads/apache-wink-1.4/dist
  ▶ 🗄 JRE System Library [JavaSE-1.6]
```

3. Now that our project is set up, let's see the following test script before
   we start:

```java
public class TestScriptUsingClientLibrary {
    public static void main(String... args){
            // Create a session with RemoteWebDriver
            // to open Firefox
        DesiredCapabilities capabilities = new
DesiredCapabilities();
        capabilities.setBrowserName("firefox");
        RemoteWebDriver remoteWD = null;
        try {
            remoteWD = new RemoteWebDriver(new
URL("http://10.172.10.1:4444/wd/hub"),capabilities);
        } catch (MalformedURLException e) {
            e.printStackTrace();
        }

            // Navigate to google Search Page
        remoteWD.get("http://www.google.com");

            // Find SearchBox Element
        WebElement element = remoteWD.findElement(By.name("q"));
```

```
                   // Type Packt Publishing in SearchBox
         element.sendKeys("Packt Publishing");

             // End the Session
             remoteWD.quit();
     }
 }
```

4. The preceding code shows how we normally add client libraries (selenium-2.33.0.jar) to our project. Now we will try to replace this and do what a client library does to communicate with the remote driver. The code for that is as follows:

```
public class TestScriptUsingJSONWireProtocol {

    public static void main(String... args){

        HttpClient httpClient = new DefaultHttpClient();
        HttpResponse response=null;
        String searchBox = null;
        String searchButton = null;
        HttpPost postMethod = null;
        HttpGet getMethod = null;
        HttpDelete deleteMethod = null;

        try {
            // Create a session with RemoteWebDriver
            // to open Firefox

            postMethod = new HttpPost("http://10.172.10.1:4444/wd/
hub/session");
            StringEntity input=null;
            JSONObject jo=new JSONObject();
            jo.put("browserName","firefox");
            JSONObject caps = new JSONObject();
            caps.put("desiredCapabilities", jo);
            System.out.println(caps.toString());
            input = new StringEntity(caps.toString());
            input.setContentEncoding("UTF-8");
            input.setContentEncoding(new BasicHeader(HTTP.CONTENT_
TYPE, "application/json"));
            postMethod.setEntity(input);

            //postMethod.set
            response = httpClient.execute(postMethod);
```

```
            //Get Sessions
        httpClient = new DefaultHttpClient();
        getMethod  = new HttpGet("http://10.172.10.1:4444/wd/hub/
sessions");
        response = httpClient.execute(getMethod);
        JSONObject json = new JSONObject(response.getEntity().
getContent());
        System.out.println(json.toString());

        String sessionId = new JSONObject(json.
getString("value").substring(1, json.getString("value").
length()-1)).getString("id");
        System.out.println("Current SessionId is: "+sessionId);


            // Navigate to Google Search Page
        httpClient = new DefaultHttpClient();
        postMethod  = new HttpPost("http:// 10.172.10.1:4444/wd/
hub/session/"+sessionId+"/url");
        jo=new JSONObject();
        jo.put("url","http://www.google.com");
        input = new StringEntity(jo.toString());
        input.setContentEncoding("UTF-8");
        input.setContentEncoding(new BasicHeader(HTTP.CONTENT_
TYPE, "application/json"));
        postMethod.setEntity(input);
        response = httpClient.execute(postMethod);

        // Find SearchBox Element
        httpClient = new DefaultHttpClient();
        postMethod = new HttpPost("http:// 10.172.10.1:4444/wd/
hub/session/"+sessionId+"/element");
        jo=new JSONObject();
        jo.put("using","name");
        jo.put("value","q");
        input = new StringEntity(jo.toString());
        input.setContentEncoding("UTF-8");
        input.setContentEncoding(new BasicHeader(HTTP.CONTENT_
TYPE, "application/json"));
        postMethod.setEntity(input);
        response = httpClient.execute(postMethod);
        json = new JSONObject(response.getEntity().getContent());
        System.out.println(json.toString());
        String searchBoxId = json.getJSONObject("value").
getString("ELEMENT");
```

```
            System.out.println("SearchBox Id is : "+ searchBoxId);

            //Click on SearchBox
            httpClient = new DefaultHttpClient();
            postMethod = new HttpPost("http:// 10.172.10.1:4444/wd/
    hub/session/"+sessionId+"/element/"+searchBoxId+"/click");
            response = httpClient.execute(postMethod);

            // Type Packt Publishing in SearchBox
            httpClient = new DefaultHttpClient();
            postMethod = new HttpPost("http:// 10.172.10.1:4444/wd/
    hub/session/"+sessionId+"/element/"+searchBoxId+"/value");
            jo=new JSONObject();
            jo.put("value",Arrays.asList(new String[]{"packt
    publishing"}));
            input = new StringEntity(jo.toString());
            input.setContentEncoding("UTF-8");
            input.setContentEncoding(new BasicHeader(HTTP.CONTENT_
    TYPE, "application/json"));
            postMethod.setEntity(input);
            response = httpClient.execute(postMethod);

            // End the Session
            httpClient = new DefaultHttpClient();
            deleteMethod = new HttpDelete("http:// 10.172.10.1:4444/
    wd/hub/session/"+sessionId);
            //response = httpClient.execute(deleteMethod);
        } catch (Exception e) {
            e.printStackTrace();
        }

    }

}
```

Each section in the original test script that uses a client library has an corresponding section in the other test script that doesn't use the client library. Each command is mapped to an API, and the necessary JSON payload is built and sent across the wire to the server or driver. That is what your client library does.

In the previous example, we have used `RemoteWebDriver`; but, you can instead talk directly to the drivers such as, Firefox Driver, IE Driver, and Chrome Driver by replacing the `RemoteWebDriver` server URL with the corresponding driver URL, that is, `http://localhost:<<port_the_driver_is_running>>`. You just have to make sure the driver is up and running.

Exploring WebDriverBackedSelenium

This section is for those test script developers who have quite a few test scripts already written in Selenium 1, also known as Selenium RC, and are planning to move to WebDriver. Moving entirely to WebDriver is a good idea theoretically, but when it comes to migrating the test scripts, it is a task that is going to keep you busy for a while, depending on how abstract your current test scripts are. The WebDriver library has provided us a class named `WebDriverBackedSelenium`, using which you can start leveraging WebDriver APIs while making sure your old Selenium 1 test scripts work fine. Before we look at `WebDriverBackedSelenium`, let us see how the good old Selenium 1 test scripts look.

If you remember, in *Chapter 1, Introducing WebDriver and WebElements*, we have discussed the history of Selenium and seen how Selenium 1 used to work by injecting the Selenium-core JavaScript into the browser and driving it, as shown in the following diagram:

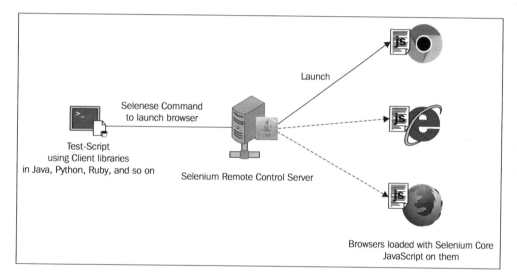

Just as with `RemoteWebDriver` test scripts, Selenium 1 tests require a Selenium server running to execute the test scripts against the target browser. It is the same `selenium-standalone-server.jar` file that we've used until now to serve as a Selenium server. A typical Selenium 1 test script will look like the following:

```
public class UsingSeleniumOne {
    public static void main(String... args){
        Selenium sel = new DefaultSelenium("localhost",4444,"*firefox",
            "http://www.google.com");
        sel.start();
```

```
sel.open("http://www.google.com.au/");
try {
    Thread.sleep(20000);
} catch (InterruptedException e) {
    e.printStackTrace();
}
sel.type("name=q", "Packt Publishing");
sel.click("name=btnG");;
    }
}
```

The `DefaultSelenium` class is the implementation of the Selenium interface. The parameters passed to it are as follows:

- The host
- The port on which the Selenium server is running
- The target browser on which the test script should be getting executed
- The base URL or the initial URL of the web application under test

Then, we start the Selenium test script execution and proceed with using Selenese commands.

Having similar test scripts in your test base, if you decide to go with Selenium 2, that is, WebDriver, and at the same time, you are sure the existing tests work fine, you have to resort to the `WebDriverBackedSelenium` class. The `WebDriverBackedSelenium` class is an extension of `DefaultSelenium`. While using `WebDriverBackedSelenium`, you should know one thing: using this class, your test scripts will still go through `DefaultSelenium`, that is, the Selenium 1 way of invoking browser and executing your tests. The main reason you modify your test scripts to use `WebDriverBackedSelenium` is because if you want to extend or implement new test scripts, from now on, you can use WebDriver APIs while not breaking the existing stuff. Let us see this with the help of an example. Let us try to convert the previous test script using `DefaultSelenium` to using `WebDriverBackedSelenium`.

The modified code will look as follows:

```
public class UsingWebDriverBackedSelenium {
    public static void main(String... args){
        WebDriver driver = new FirefoxDriver();
        String baseUrl = "http://www.google.com.au/";
        Selenium sel = new WebDriverBackedSelenium(driver, baseUrl);

        sel.open("http://www.google.com.au/");
        try {
```

```
        Thread.sleep(20000);
    } catch (InterruptedException e) {
        e.printStackTrace();
    }
    sel.type("name=q", "Packt Publishing");
    sel.click("name=btnG");
    }
}
```

In the Selenium 1 code, consider the following lines of code:

```
Selenium sel = new DefaultSelenium("localhost",4444,"*firefox",
        "http://www.google.com");
sel.start();
```

They will be replaced with:

```
WebDriver driver = new FirefoxDriver();
String baseUrl = "http://www.google.com.au/";
Selenium sel = new WebDriverBackedSelenium(driver, baseUrl);
```

From that point forward, the rest of the test script commands will go to the `DefaultSelenium` instance via the `WebDriverBackedSelenium` class as it extends the `DefaultSelenium` class. At this point, if you want to extend your test scripts to use some of the WebDriver APIs, you can use the following method to get the underlying WebDriver:

```
public WebDriver getWrappedDriver()
```

Using this method, you can handle the WebDriver instance, which is the same instance of Selenium that our test script has used so far to execute its commands. Once you get a handle on the WebDriver instance, you can invoke various WebDriver APIs. So, to reiterate, replacing the `DefaultSelenium` code with the `WebDriverBackedSelenium` code will not make your existing test script commands use WebDriver APIs; they still go through the Selenium 1 libraries, and you need to replace those methods with the WebDriver API methods. However, using the `getWrappedDriver()` method of `WebDriverBackedSelenium`, you can extend your test script to use the WebDriver APIs.

You should look forward to migrating your test scripts from using Selenium 1 methods to WebDriver APIs. Some of the advantages of migrating test scripts from using Selenium 1 to Selenium 2 are as follows:

- Better object-oriented APIs in WebDriver compared with Selenium 1 APIs
- Better emulation of user actions of WebDriver than that of Selenium 1
- Most browsers support WebDriver over Selenium 1

Summary

Thus, we have seen what `RemoteWebDriver` is and how to execute test scripts remotely on a different machine using the `RemoteWebDriver` server and the `RemoteWebDriver` client. This type of execution of test scripts is something you, as a test script developer, will come across often. So, mastering it will definitely be useful.

You have also seen what the JSON wire protocol is and the work our client libraries do behind the scenes to send and receive our requests and responses to and from the drivers. Replacing them with your code is definitely not an option, but knowing how they work and the API reference they use is definitely useful.

Finally, you now know how to enhance your existing test scripts and test frameworks using Selenium 1 to work with WebDriver APIs using `WebDriverBackedSelenium`.

In the next chapter, we will see what a Selenium Grid is and how it works.

8

Understanding Selenium Grid

Now that we know what Remote WebDriver is and how it works, we are ready to learn about Selenium Grid. In this chapter, we will cover the following topics:

- Why we need Selenium Grid
- What Selenium Grid is
- How we can use Selenium Grid
- Test cases using Selenium Grid
- Configuring Selenium Grid

Exploring Selenium Grid

Let us try to understand why we need Selenium Grid by analyzing a scenario. You have a web application that you have to test on the IE 8 browser on Windows XP platform, IE 10 browser on Windows 8, Chrome on Mac OS X, and Firefox on Red Hat Linux machines. This can be achieved by altering your test case to point to the Remote WebDriver running on the target platform (that is, Windows XP, Windows 8, Mac, or Linux), as shown in the following code:

```
WebDriver driver = new RemoteWebDriver(new URL("http://<WindowsXP-
    ip>:4444/wd/hub"), capabilities);
WebDriver driver = new RemoteWebDriver(new URL("http://<Windows8-
    ip>:4444/wd/hub"), capabilities);
WebDriver driver = new RemoteWebDriver(new URL("http://<MacOS-
    ip>:4444/wd/hub"), capabilities);
WebDriver driver = new RemoteWebDriver(new URL("http://<Linux-
    ip>:4444/wd/hub"), capabilities);
```

This is something we have learned in the previous chapter. If you observe, in the preceding code, your test scripts are tightly coupled to the machines that host the target platform and the target browsers. If the Windows 8 host changes, you should refactor your test script to handle that. This is not an ideal way of designing your tests. The focus of your test scripts should be on the functionality of your web application and not on the infrastructure that is used to execute these test scripts. There should be a central point to manage all the different environments. To solve this, we make use of Selenium Grid.

Selenium Grid is a testing infrastructure with several different platforms (such as Windows, Mac, Linux, and so on) for your tests to execute, and these platforms are managed from a central point. The central point known as **hub**, has the information of all the different testing platforms known as **nodes**, and assigns these nodes to execute tests whenever the test scripts request them. The following diagram shows what a Selenium Grid looks like:

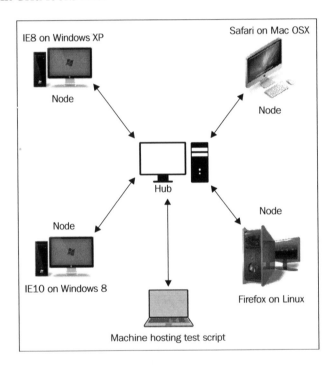

In the preceding diagram, there is one hub, four nodes of different platforms, and the machine where your test scripts are located. The test script will communicate with the hub and request for a target platform to be executed. The hub assigns a node with the target platform to the test script. The node executes the test script and sends the result back to the hub, which in turn forwards the results to the test script. This is what Selenium Grid looks like and how works at a high level.

Now that we have seen how Selenium Grid works theorectically, let us see what works as hubs and nodes in it. Fortunately, as we are dealing with Selenium Grid 2, we can use the same Remote WebDriver server that we used in the previous chapter to work as Selenium Grid as well. If you remember, we have used `selenium-server-standalone-2.33.0.jar` to start as a Remote WebDriver. We can use the same JAR file to be started in the hub mode on the hub machine, and a copy of the JAR file can be started in the node mode on the node machine. In Selenium Grid 1, Remote WebDriver and Selenium Grid jars used to be different. Now, both those functionalities are combined into one JAR. Try executing the following command on your JAR file:

```
java -jar selenium-server-standalone-2.33.0.jar -help
```

The following output shows how to use the server in a grid environment:

```
-----------------------------------
To use in a grid environment :
-----------------------------------
Usage :
  -hubConfig:
    (hub) a JSON file following grid2 format that defines the hub
      properties.

  -nodeTimeout:
    (node) <XXXX>  the timeout in seconds before the hub
      automatically ends a test that hasn't had any activity in the
      last X seconds. The browser will be released for another test to
      use. This typically takes care of the client crashes.

  -throwOnCapabilityNotPresent:
    (hub) <true | false> default to true. If true, the hub will
      reject test requests right away if no proxy is currently
      registered that can host that capability. Set it to false to have
      the request queued until a node supporting the capability is
      added to the grid.

  -maxSession:
    (node) max number of tests that can run at the same time on the
      node, independently of the browser used.
```

`-hub`:

> (node) <http://localhost:4444/grid/register> : the url that will be used to post the registration request. This option takes precedence over -hubHost and -hubPort options.

`-hubPort`:

> (node) <xxxx> : the port listened by a hub the registration request should be sent to. Default to 4444. Option -hub takes precedence over this option.

`-registerCycle`:

> (node) how often in ms the node will try to register itself again. Allow to restart the hub without having to restart the nodes.

`-capabilityMatcher`:

> (hub) a class implementing the CapabilityMatcher interface. Defaults to org.openqa.grid.internal.utils.DefaultCapabilityMatcher. Specify the logic the hub will follow to define if a request can be assigned to a node. Change this class if you want to have the matching process use regular expression instead of exact match for the version of the browser for instance. All the nodes of a grid instance will use the same matcher, defined by the registry.

`-port`:

> (hub & node) <xxxx> : the port the remote/hub will listen on. Default to 4444.

`-hubHost`:

> (node) <IP | hostname> : the host address of a hub the registration request should be sent to. Default to localhost. Option -hub takes precedence over this option.

`-newSessionWaitTimeout`:

> (hub) <XXXX>. Default to no timeout (-1) the time in ms after

which a new test waiting for a node to become available will time out.When that happens, the test will throw an exception before starting a browser.

-nodePolling:

(node) how often the hub checks if the node is still alive.

-host:

(hub & node) <IP | hostname> : usually not needed and determined automatically. For exotic network configuration, network with VPN, specifying the host might be necessary.

-unregisterIfStillDownAfter:

(node) in ms. If the node remains down for more than unregisterIfStillDownAfter millisec, it will disappear from the hub.Default is 1min.

-cleanupCycle:

(node) <XXXX> in ms. How often a proxy will check for timed out thread.

-nodeConfig:

(node) a JSON file following grid2 format that defines the node properties.

-prioritizer:

(hub) a class implementing the Prioritizer interface. Default to null (no priority = FIFO).Specify a custom prioritizer if you need the grid to process the tests from the CI, or the IE tests first for instance.

-servlets:

(hub & node) <com.mycompany.MyServlet,com.mycompany.MyServlet2> to register a new servlet on the hub/node. The servlet will accessible under the path /grid/admin/MyServlet /grid/admin/MyServlet2

```
-proxy:
   (node) the class that will be used to represent the node. By
      default org.openqa.grid.selenium.proxy.DefaultRemoteProxy.


-browserTimeout:
   (hub/node) The timeout in seconds a browser can hang


-grid1Yml:
   (hub) a YML file following grid1 format.


-role:
   <hub|node> (default is no grid, just run an RC/webdriver server).
      When launching a node, the parameters will be forwarded to the
      server on the node, so you can use something like -role node
-trustAllSSLCertificates.  In that case, the SeleniumServer will
      be launch with the trustallSSLCertificates option.
```

You will see two options: **To use as a standalone server**, which acts as a Remote WebDriver, and **To use in a grid environment,** which describes Selenium Grid. In this chapter, we will use this JAR file as a Selenium Grid.

Understanding the hub

The hub is the central point of a Selenium Grid. It has a registry of all the available nodes that are part of a particular grid. The hub is again a Selenium server running in the hub mode listening on port 4444 of a machine by default. The test scripts will try to connect to the hub on this port, just as any Remote WebDriver. The hub will take care of rerouting the test script traffic to the appropriate test platform node. Let us see how we can start a hub node. Navigate to the location where you have your Selenium server jar file and execute the following command:

```
java -jar selenium-server-standalone-2.33.0.jar -role hub
```

Doing this will start your server in the hub mode. By default, the server starts listening on port 4444; however, you can start your server on the port of your choice. Suppose you want to start the server on port 1111; it can be done as follows:

```
java -jar selenium-server-standalone-2.33.0.jar
  -role hub  -port 1111
```

The following screenshot shows the console output of the Grid Hub being started on port 1111:

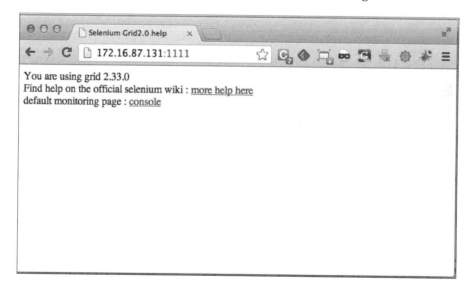

All the test scripts should connect to the hub on this port. Now, launch your browser and connect to the machine that is hosting your hub on port 1111. Here, the machine that is hosting my hub has the IP address 172.16.87.131.

What you should see on your browser is shown in the following screenshot:

It shows the version of the server that is being used as the Grid Hub. Now, click the **Console** link to navigate to the Grid Console:

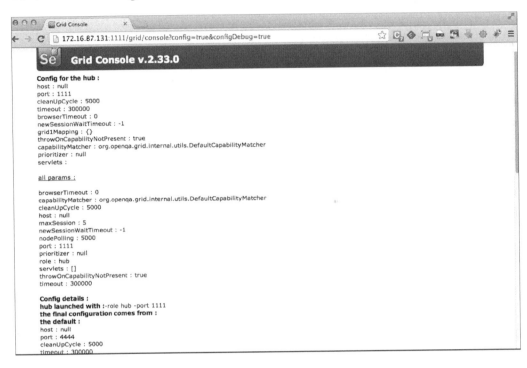

As you can see, the page talks about many configuration parameters. We will discuss these configuration parameters in the *Configuring Selenium Grid* section. So, until now, you have learned how to start a grid on a port and listen for connections.

Understanding the node

As our hub is up and running, it's now time to start the node. Here, my node is a Mac OS X platform with Chrome, Firefox, and Safari installed on it. So, if any test script requests the hub for a Mac OS X platform, the hub will choose this node. Let us see how we can start the node. The command to start the node and register with the hub is as follows.

```
java -jar selenium-server-standalone-2.33.0.jar -role node -hub
    http://172.16.87.131:1111/grid/register
```

This will start the Selenium server in the node mode and register this node with the already started hub. If you go back to the Grid Console on the browser, you will see the following screenshot:

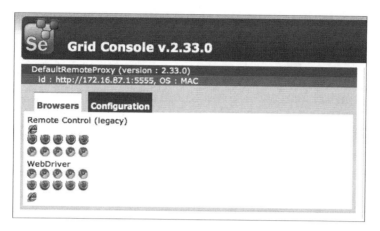

The preceding screenshot shows the node URL **http://172.16.87.1:5555**, which in this case is running on the MAC platform. By default, the number of browsers listed for every node is 11: five for Firefox, 5 for Chrome, and 1 for IE. This can be overridden by specifying the `-browser` option, which we will see in the *Configuring Selenium Grid* section shortly. Also, this grid can work with both Selenium RC and Selenium WebDriver test scripts. Now, click the **Configuration** tab of the node in the console UI. The default configuration with which the node is registered with the hub can be seen in the following screenshot:

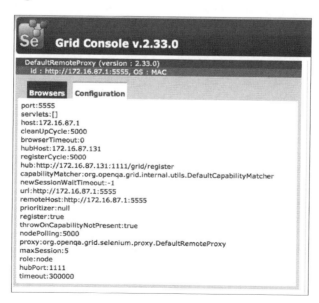

Similarly, start another node that is Windows-based and register with the same hub using the same command used to start the node on Mac. Now, go back to the Console UI to see the two registered nodes, as shown in the following screenshot:

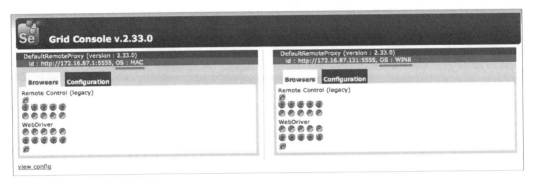

Modifying the existing test script to use Selenium Grid

Until now, we have seen test scripts that run on our local machines or on Remote WebDriver servers. Executing test scripts on Selenium Grid is very similar to executing tests on Remote WebDriver, except that you will mention the platform details as well for Grid.

Let us look at a test script that uses the Remote WebDriver server:

```
public class UsingRemoteWebDriver {
  public static void main(String... args){
    DesiredCapabilities capabilities = new DesiredCapabilities();
    capabilities.setBrowserName("firefox");
    RemoteWebDriver remoteWD = null;
    try {
      remoteWD = new RemoteWebDriver(new URL("http://<remote-
        webdriver-ip>:4444/wd/hub"),capabilities);
    } catch (MalformedURLException e) {
      e.printStackTrace();
    }
    remoteWD.get("http://www.google.com");
    WebElement element = remoteWD.findElement(By.name("q"));
    element.sendKeys("Packt Publishing");
    remoteWD.quit();
  }
}
```

Let us modify the test script to use the Selenium Grid Hub that we started earlier:

```java
public class UsingSeleniumGrid {
  public static void main(String... args){
    DesiredCapabilities capabilities = new DesiredCapabilities();
    capabilities.setBrowserName("firefox");
    RemoteWebDriver remoteWD = null;
    try {
      remoteWD = new RemoteWebDriver(
      new URL("http://172.16.87.131:1111/wd/hub"),
      capabilities);
    } catch (MalformedURLException e) {
      e.printStackTrace();
    }
    remoteWD.get("http://www.google.com");
    WebElement element = remoteWD.findElement(By.name("q"));
    element.sendKeys("Packt Publishing");
    remoteWD.quit();
  }
}
```

There is absolutely no difference in the code as long as you only care for the browser (Firefox, in this case), and the platform the test script is going to execute is not important for you. But if you want your test script to be executed on a Mac OS platform and on the Firefox browser, you have to add that capability in the test script. The modified version of the above test script would look as follows:

```java
public class UsingSeleniumGrid {
  public static void main(String... args){
    DesiredCapabilities capabilities
      = new DesiredCapabilities();
    capabilities.setPlatform(Platform.MAC);
    capabilities.setBrowserName("firefox");
    RemoteWebDriver remoteWD = null;
    try {
      remoteWD = new RemoteWebDriver(
      new   URL("http://172.16.87.131:1111/wd/hub"),
      capabilities);
    } catch (MalformedURLException e) {
      e.printStackTrace();
    }
    remoteWD.get("http://www.google.com");
    WebElement element = remoteWD.findElement(By.name("q"));
```

```
    element.sendKeys("Packt Publishing");
    remoteWD.quit();
  }
}
```

Now, try executing the above test script and observe the log output of the hub and the node. The output log of the hub is as follows:

```
INFO: Got a request to create a new session: {platform=MAC, browserName=firefox}
Oct 20, 2013 12:25:19 PM org.openqa.grid.internal.ProxySet getNewSession
INFO: Available nodes: [host :http://172.16.87.1:5555 time out : 300000, host :http://172.16.87.131:5555 time out
: 300000]
Oct 20, 2013 12:25:19 PM org.openqa.grid.internal.BaseRemoteProxy getNewSession
INFO: Trying to create a new session on node host :http://172.16.87.1:5555 time out : 300000
Oct 20, 2013 12:25:19 PM org.openqa.grid.internal.TestSlot getNewSession
INFO: Trying to create a new session on test slot {seleniumProtocol=WebDriver, platform=MAC, browserName=firefox,
maxInstances=5}
```

The sequence of steps that happens at the hub end is as follows:

1. The hub gets a request to create a new session for `platform=MAC`, `browserName=firefox`.

2. It verifies the available nodes that match the `capabilities` request.

3. If available, it creates a new session with the node host; if not, it rejects the request from the test script saying that the desired capabilities don't match with any of the registered nodes.

4. If a session is created with the node host in the preceding step, create a new test slot session and hand over the test script to the node.

Similarly, the output you should see on the Console log of the node is as follows:

```
12:25:19.516 INFO - Executing: [new session: [platform=MAC, browserName=firefox]] at URL: /session)
12:25:19.595 INFO - Creating a new session for Capabilities [{platform=MAC, browserName=firefox}]
12:27:04.509 INFO - Done: /session
12:27:04.557 INFO - Executing: org.openqa.selenium.remote.server.handler.GetSessionCapabilities@2e027538 at URL: /session/a7f1d8f6-3719-43aa-ac08-f767283b1eab)
12:27:04.557 INFO - Done: /session/a7f1d8f6-3719-43aa-ac08-f767283b1eab
12:27:04.650 INFO - Executing: [get: http://www.google.com] at URL: /session/a7f1d8f6-3719-43aa-ac08-f767283b1eab/url)
12:27:07.775 INFO - Done: /session/a7f1d8f6-3719-43aa-ac08-f767283b1eab/url
12:27:07.791 INFO - Executing: [find element: By.name: q] at URL: /session/a7f1d8f6-3719-43aa-ac08-f767283b1eab/element)
12:27:08.059 INFO - Done: /session/a7f1d8f6-3719-43aa-ac08-f767283b1eab/element
12:27:08.113 INFO - Executing: [send keys: 0 org.openqa.selenium.support.events.EventFiringWebDriver$EventFiringWebElement@5a49ef92, [Packt Publishing]] at URL: /sess)
on/a7f1d8f6-3719-43aa-ac08-f767283b1eab/element/0/value)
12:27:08.210 INFO - Executing: [delete session: a7f1d8f6-3719-43aa-ac08-f767283b1eab] at URL: /session/a7f1d8f6-3719-43aa-ac08-f767283b1eab)
12:27:08.217 INFO - Done: /session/a7f1d8f6-3719-43aa-ac08-f767283b1eab
12:27:08.294 INFO - Done: /session/a7f1d8f6-3719-43aa-ac08-f767283b1eab
```

The sequence of steps is performed on the node host is as follows:

1. The node host creates a new session with the requested desired capabilities. This will launch the browser.

2. It executes the test script's steps on the launched browser.

3. It ends the session and forwards the result to the hub, which in turn sends it to the test script.

Requesting for nonregistered capabilities

The hub will reject the request from the test script when the test script asks for a capability that is not registered with the hub. Let's modify the preceding test script to request for the Opera browser instead of Firefox. The test script should look as follows:

```
ublic class UsingSeleniumGrid {
  public static void main(String... args){
    DesiredCapabilities capabilities = new DesiredCapabilities();
    capabilities.setPlatform(Platform.MAC);
    capabilities.setBrowserName("opera");
    RemoteWebDriver remoteWD = null;
    try {
      remoteWD = new RemoteWebDriver(
      new    URL("http://172.16.87.131:1111/wd/hub"),
      capabilities);
    } catch (MalformedURLException e) {
      e.printStackTrace();
    }
    remoteWD.get("http://www.google.com");
    WebElement element = remoteWD.findElement(By.name("q"));
    element.sendKeys("Packt Publishing");
    remoteWD.quit();
  }
}
```

The hub checks if there is any node matching the desired capabilities. If it doesn't find any (as in this case), it will reject the request from the test script by throwing an exception, as shown in the following screenshot:

```
Exception in thread "main" org.openqa.selenium.WebDriverException: Error forwarding the new session cannot find :
{platform=MAC, browserName=opera}
Command duration or timeout: 141 milliseconds
Build info: version: '2.33.0', revision: '4e90c97', time: '2013-05-22 15:33:32'
System info: os.name: 'Windows 8', os.arch: 'x86', os.version: '6.2', java.version: '1.7.0_21'
Driver info: org.openqa.selenium.remote.RemoteWebDriver
    at sun.reflect.NativeConstructorAccessorImpl.newInstance0(Native Method)
    at sun.reflect.NativeConstructorAccessorImpl.newInstance(Unknown Source)
    at sun.reflect.DelegatingConstructorAccessorImpl.newInstance(Unknown Source)
```

Queuing up the request if the node is busy

By default, you can send five test script requests to any node. Although it is possible to change that configuration, let us see what happens when a node is already serving five requests, and you fire up another request for that node via the hub. The hub will keep polling the node until it gets a free test slot from the node. The test scripts are made to wait all this while. The log output you will see on the console for the sixth request would be as follows:

```
Oct 20, 2013 1:33:42 PM org.openqa.grid.internal.BaseRemoteProxy getNewSession
INFO: Trying to create a new session on node host :http://172.16.87.131:5555 time out : 300000
Oct 20, 2013 1:33:42 PM org.openqa.grid.internal.BaseRemoteProxy getNewSession
INFO: Node host :http://172.16.87.131:5555 time out : 300000 has no matching capability
Oct 20, 2013 1:33:42 PM org.openqa.grid.internal.BaseRemoteProxy getNewSession
INFO: Trying to create a new session on node host :http://172.16.87.1:5555 time out : 300000
Oct 20, 2013 1:33:42 PM org.openqa.grid.internal.BaseRemoteProxy getNewSession
INFO: Node host :http://172.16.87.1:5555 time out : 300000 has no free slots
```

The hub says there no free slots for the sixth session to be established with the same node, and the Grid Console UI on the browser says that too, as shown in the following screenshot:

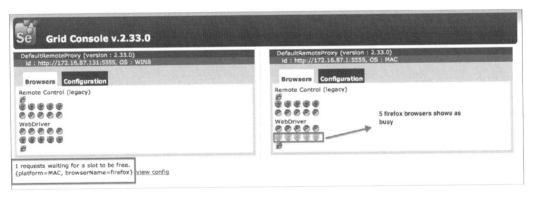

Meanwhile, on the node host, the node tries to create sessions for the five requests and starts executing the test scripts as shown in the following screenshot:

```
13:10:19.632 INFO - starting auto register thread. Will try to register every 5000 ms.
13:10:19.632 INFO - Registering the node to hub :http://172.16.87.131:1111/grid/register
13:32:29.239 INFO - Executing: [new session: {platform=MAC, browserName=firefox}] at URL: /session)
13:32:29.249 INFO - Creating a new session for Capabilities [{platform=MAC, browserName=firefox}]
13:32:33.312 INFO - Executing: [new session: {platform=MAC, browserName=firefox}] at URL: /session)
13:32:33.313 INFO - Creating a new session for Capabilities [{platform=MAC, browserName=firefox}]
13:32:37.925 INFO - Executing: [new session: {platform=MAC, browserName=firefox}] at URL: /session)
13:32:37.926 INFO - Creating a new session for Capabilities [{platform=MAC, browserName=firefox}]
13:32:43.075 INFO - Executing: [new session: {platform=MAC, browserName=firefox}] at URL: /session)
13:32:43.076 INFO - Creating a new session for Capabilities [{platform=MAC, browserName=firefox}]
13:32:47.207 INFO - Executing: [new session: {platform=MAC, browserName=firefox}] at URL: /session)
13:32:47.207 INFO - Creating a new session for Capabilities [{platform=MAC, browserName=firefox}]
```

Upon creating the sessions, five Firefox windows are launched and the test scripts are executed on them as shown in the following screenshot:

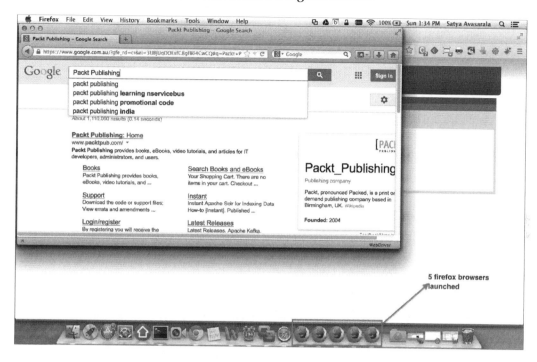

Upon serving the five test script requests, the hub will establish the waiting sixth session with the node, and the sixth request will be served.

Dealing with two nodes with matching capabilities

When two nodes of the same capabilities are registered with a hub, a test script request receives the node that is registered first with the hub. If the first registered node is busy handling other test script requests, only then the hub directs the request to the second node with matching requested capabilities.

Configuring Selenium Grid

There are many configuration options that Selenium Grid provides to control the behavior of a node and a hub while you execute your test scripts. We will discuss them here in this section.

Specifying node configuration parameters

In this section, we will go through the configuration parameters for a node.

Setting supported browsers by a node

As we saw earlier, when we register a node with a hub, by default the node is shown as supporting five instances of the Firefox browser, five instances of the Chrome browser, and one instance of Internet Explorer, irrespective of whether or not the node actually supports them. But to register your node with the browsers of your choice, Selenium Grid provides a `-browser` option, using which we can achieve this.

Let us say we want our node to be registered as supporting Firefox, Chrome, and Safari browsers; we can do that using the following command:

```
java -jar selenium-server-standalone-2.33.0.jar -role node -hub
http://172.16.87.131:1111/grid/register -browser browserName=firefox
-browser browserName=chrome -browser browserName=safari
```

The Grid Console looks as shown in the following screenshot:

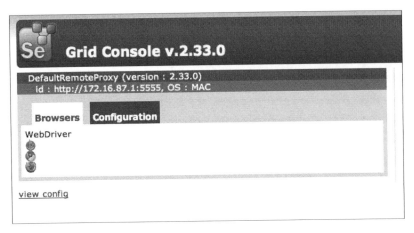

Setting node timeouts

This parameter is set when registering a node with a hub. The value provided to these parameters is the time in seconds that a hub can actually wait before it terminates a test script execution on a node if the test script doesn't perform any kind of activity on the node.

The command to configure your node with a node timeout is as follows:

```
java -jar selenium-server-standalone-2.33.0.jar -role node -hub
   http://172.16.87.131:1111/grid/register -nodeTimeout 300
```

Here, we have registered a node with a node timeout value of 300 seconds. So, the hub will terminate the test script if it doesn't perform any activity on the node for more than 300 seconds.

Setting the limit on browser instances

We have seen that by default, there are 11 instances of browsers getting registered for a node. We have seen how to register our own browser. In this section, we will see how many instances of those browsers we can allow in our node. For this to be controlled, Selenium Grid comes out with a configuration parameter called maxInstances, using which we can specify how many instances of a particular browser we want our node to provide. The command to do that is as follows:

```
java -jar selenium-server-standalone-2.33.0.jar -role node -hub
http://172.16.87.131:1111/grid/register -browser "browserName=firefox,max
Instances=3" -browser "browserName=chrome,maxInstances=3" -browser "brows
erName=safari,maxInstances=1"
```

Here, we are registering a node that provides three instances of Firefox, three instances of Chrome, and one instance of Safari. The Grid Console will look as follows:

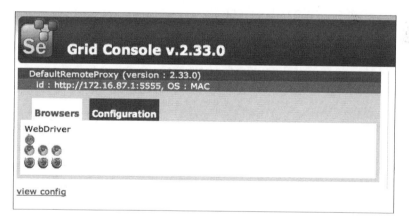

Reregistering the node automatically

If the hub crashes or restarts after a node registers to it, all the information of the nodes that are already registered is lost. Going back to each of the nodes and reregistering them manually would prove to be tedious. The impact will be even more if we haven't realized that the hub has restarted because all the test scripts would fail as a result. So, to handle this kind of situation, Selenium Grid provides a configuration parameter to a node through which we can specify the node to reregister itself automatically to the hub after a specified amount of time. If not specified, the default time of reregistration is five seconds. This way, we really don't have to worry; even if the hub crashes or restarts, our node will try to reregister every five seconds.

If you want to modify this time, the configuration parameter to deal with is `registerCycle`. The command to specify is as follows:

```
java -jar selenium-server-standalone-2.33.0.jar -role node -hub
    http://172.16.87.131:1111/grid/register -registerCycle 10000
```

The output you will see on the node log console during startup is as follows:

```
17:47:01.231 INFO - starting auto register thread. Will try to
    register every 10000 ms.
17:47:01.232 INFO - Registering the node to hub
    :http://172.16.87.131:1111/grid/register
```

Setting node health-check time

Using this configuration parameter, we can specify how frequently the hub can poll a node for its availability. The parameter that is used to achieve this is `nodePolling`. By specifying this to the hub at the node level, each node can specify its own frequency at which it can be health checked. The command to configure your node is as follows:

```
java -jar selenium-server-standalone-2.33.0.jar -role node -hub
    http://172.16.87.131:1111/grid/register -nodePolling 10
```

Now, the hub will poll this node every 10 seconds to check its availability.

Unregistering an unavailable node

Although the `nodePolling` configuration will make the hub poll the node often, the `unregisterIfStillDownAfter` configuration will let the hub unregister the node if the poll doesn't produce an expected result. Let's say a node is down, and the hub tries to poll the node and is unable to connect to it. At this point, how long the hub is going to poll for the availability of the node is determined by the `unregisterIfStillDownAfter` parameter. Beyond this time, the hub will and unregister the node.

The command to do that is as follows:

```
.java -jar selenium-server-standalone-2.33.0.jar -role node -hub
   http://172.16.87.131:1111/grid/register -nodePolling 5 -
   unregistIfStillDownAfter 20000
```

Here, the hub will poll the node every five seconds; if the node is down, the polling will continue for 20 seconds, that is, the hub will poll four times and then unregister the node from the grid.

Setting the browser timeout

This configuration is to let the node know how long it should wait before it ends a test script session when the browser seems to hang. Beyond this time, the node will abort the browser session and start with the next waiting test script. The configuration parameter for this is `browserTimeout`. The command to specify that is as follows:

```
java -jar selenium-server-standalone-2.33.0.jar -role node -hub
   http://172.16.87.131:1111/grid/register -browserTimeout 60
```

So, these are the some of the configuration parameters that you can specify at the node end and have a better control over the Selenium Grid environment.

Hub configuration parameters

This section talks about some of the configuration parameters on the hub side.

Waiting for a match of desired capability

As we saw earlier, when the test script asks for a test platform with some desired capability, the hub will reject the request if it doesn't find a suitable node with the desired capability.

Altering the value for the `throwOnCapabilityNotPresent` parameter can alter this behavior. By default, it is set to `true`, which means the hub will reject the request if it doesn't find a suitable node with that capability. But setting this parameter to `false` will queue the request, and the hub will wait until a node with that capability is added to the grid. The command that has to be invoked is as follows:

```
java -jar selenium-server-standalone-2.33.0.jar -role hub -port 1111
-throwOnCapabilityNotPresent false
```

Now, the hub will not reject the request but will place the request in a queue and wait until the requested platform is available.

Customized CapabilityMatcher

By default, the hub will use the `org.openqa.grid.internal.utils.` `DefaultCapabilityMatcher` class to match the node that is requested. If you do not like the implementation logic of the `DefaultCapabilityMatcher` class, you can extend the class, implement your own `CapabilityMatcher` class, and provide your own logic in it.

Once developed, you can ask the hub to use that class to match the capabilities with the nodes using a configuration parameter named `capabilityMatcher`. The command to achieve this is as follows:

```
java -jar selenium-server-standalone-2.33.0.jar -role hub
-port 1111
-capabilityMatcher com.yourcomp.CustomCapabilityMatcher
```

The hub will use the logic defined in your `CustomCapabilityMatcher` class to identify the nodes to be assigned to the test script requests.

WaitTimeout for a new session

When a capability-matched node is busy executing other test scripts, the latest test script will wait for the node to be available. By default, there is no wait timeout; that is, the test script will wait for the node to be available indefinitely. To alter that behavior and to let the test script throw an exception if it doesn't get the node within a limited time, Selenium Grid opens a configuration that enables the test script to do so. The configuration parameter controlling that behavior is `newSessionWaitTimeout`. The command for that is as follows:

```
java -jar selenium-server-standalone-2.33.0.jar -role hub
-port 1111 -newSessionWaitTimeout 120000
```

Here, the test script will wait for two minutes before it throws an exception saying it couldn't obtain a node to execute itself.

Different ways to specify the configuration

There are two ways to specify the configuration parameter to the Selenium Grid's hub and node. The first one is what we have been seeing all this time; that is, specifying the configuration parameters over the command line. The second way of doing it is providing a JSON file that contains all these configuration parameters.

A node configuration file (say `nodeConfig.json`)—a typical JSON file having all the configuration parameters—looks something similar to the following:

```json
{
  "capabilities":
      [
        {
          "browserName": "*firefox",
          "maxInstances": 5,
          "seleniumProtocol": "Selenium"
        },
        {

          "browserName": "*googlechrome",
          "maxInstances": 5,
          "seleniumProtocol": "Selenium"
        },
        {

          "browserName": "*iexplore",
          "maxInstances": 1,
          "seleniumProtocol": "Selenium"
        },
        {

          "browserName": "firefox",
          "maxInstances": 5,
          "seleniumProtocol": "WebDriver"
        },
        {

          "browserName": "chrome",
          "maxInstances": 5,
          "seleniumProtocol": "WebDriver"
        },
        {

          "browserName": "internet explorer",
          "maxInstances": 1,
          "seleniumProtocol": "WebDriver"
        }
      ],
  "configuration":
  {
    "proxy": "org.openqa.grid.selenium.proxy.DefaultRemoteProxy",
    "maxSession": 5,
    "port": 5555,
    "host": ip,
    "register": true,
    "registerCycle": 5000,
    "hubPort": 4444,
```

```
    "hubHost": ip
  }
}
```

Similarly, a hub configuration file (`hubConfig.json`) looks as follows:

```
{
  "host": null,
  "port": 4444,
  "newSessionWaitTimeout": -1,
  "servlets" : [],
  "prioritizer": null,
  "capabilityMatcher":
    "org.openqa.grid.internal.utils.DefaultCapabilityMatcher",
  "throwOnCapabilityNotPresent": true,
  "nodePolling": 5000,
  "cleanUpCycle": 5000,
  "timeout": 300000,
  "browserTimeout": 0,
  "maxSession": 5
}
```

Once these files are configured, they can be provided to the node and hub using the following command:

```
java -jar selenium-server-standalone.jar -role node -nodeConfig
  nodeconfig.json
```

```
java -jar selenium-server-standalone.jar -role hub -hubConfig
  hubconfig.json
```

This way, you can specify the configuration of your hub and node using JSON files.

Summary

In this chapter, you have seen what a Selenium Grid is, how a hub and node will work, and more importantly, understood how to configure your Selenium Grid to have a better control over the environment and infrastructure. Having a good setup of Selenium Grid will help you validate your test scripts on various and multiple environments very easily, and so you can execute your test scripts in parallel.

In the next chapter, we will discuss effective ways of designing your test automation framework using a design pattern called PageObject pattern, which is supported by WebDriver.

9

Understanding PageObject Pattern

Until now, we have seen various APIs of WebDriver and learned how to use them to accomplish various actions on the web application we're testing. We created many test scripts that use these APIs and are executed on a daily or weekly basis. One big challenge that you have to deal with, regarding these test scripts, is maintainability. In this chapter, we will cover the following topics:

- What is the PageObject pattern design?
- Good practices for designing PageObjects
- Extensions to the PageObject pattern
- An end-to-end example

A decently written test script would work just fine as long as the target web application doesn't change. But once one or more pages in your web application change, you as a test script writer shouldn't be in a position where you have to refactor your test scripts at a hundred different places. Let us see that with an example. We will try to go through this chapter by working on a WordPress blog. Before we start, I would like you to create a WordPress blog (`http://wordpress.com/about`) or use one of your existing ones.

Creating test cases for our WordPress blog

Here, we are using a WordPress blog with the following URL `http://pageobjectpattern.wordpress.com/`. Let us create three test cases for it before we start talking about the PageObject pattern.

Test case 1 – Adding a new post to our WordPress blog

The following test script will log in to the Admin portal of our WordPress blog and add a new blog post:

```
public class TestAddNewPost {
    public static void main(String... args) {
        WebDriver driver = new FirefoxDriver();
        // Login to Admin portal
        driver.get("http://pageobjectpattern.wordpress.com/wp-admin");
        WebElement email = driver.findElement(By.id("user_login"));
        WebElement pwd = driver.findElement(By.id("user_pass"));
        WebElement submit = driver.findElement(By.id("wp-submit"));
        email.sendKeys("pageobjectpattern@gmail.com");
        pwd.sendKeys("webdriver123");
        submit.click();
        // Go to AllPosts page
        driver.get("http://pageobjectpattern.wordpress.com/wp-
admin/edit.php");
        // Add New Post
        WebElement addNewPost = driver.findElement(By.linkText("Add
New"));
        addNewPost.click();
        // Add New Post's Content
        driver.switchTo().frame("content_ifr");
        WebElement postBody = driver.findElement(By.id("tinymce"));
        postBody.sendKeys("This is description");
        driver.switchTo().defaultContent();
        WebElement title = driver.findElement(By.id("title"));
        title.click();
        title.sendKeys("My First Post");
        // Publish the Post
        WebElement publish = driver.findElement(By.id("publish"));
        publish.click();
    }
}
```

The following is the sequence of steps that the preceding code performs:

1. Log in to the WordPress Admin portal.

2. Go to the **All Posts** page.

3. Click on the **Add New** post button.

4. Add a new post by providing the title and description.

5. Publish the post.

Test case 2 – Deleting a post from our WordPress blog

The following test script will log in to our WordPress blog and delete an existing post:

```
public class TestDeletePost {
    public static void main(String... args) {
        WebDriver driver = new FirefoxDriver();
        // Login to Admin portal
driver.get("http://pageobjectpattern.wordpress.com/wp-admin");
        WebElement email =
driver.findElement(By.id("user_login"));
        WebElement pwd =
driver.findElement(By.id("user_pass"));
        WebElement submit = driver.findElement(By.id("wp-
submit"));
        email.sendKeys("pageobjectpattern@gmail.com");
        pwd.sendKeys("webdriver123");
        submit.click();
        // Go to a All Posts page
driver.get("http://pageobjectpattern.wordpress.com/wp-
admin/edit.php");
        // Click on the post to be deleted
        WebElement post = driver.findElement(By.linkText("My
First Post"));
        post.click();
        // Delete Post
        WebElement publish = driver.findElement(By.linkText("Move
to Trash"));
        publish.click();
    }
}
```

The following is the sequence of steps that the preceding test script follows to delete a post:

1. Log in to the WordPress Admin portal.

2. Go to the **All Posts** page.

3. Click on the post to be deleted.

4. Delete the post.

Test case 3 – Counting the number of posts on our WordPress blog

The following test script will count all the posts currently available on our WordPress blog:

```
public class TestPostsCount {
    public static void main(String... args){
        WebDriver driver = new FirefoxDriver();
            // Login to Admin portal
driver.get("http://pageobjectpattern.wordpress.com/wp-admin");
            WebElement email =
driver.findElement(By.id("user_login"));
            WebElement pwd =
driver.findElement(By.id("user_pass"));
            WebElement submit = driver.findElement(By.id("wp-
submit"));
            email.sendKeys("pageobjectpattern@gmail.com");
            pwd.sendKeys("webdriver123");
            submit.click();
            // Count the number of posts.
            driver.get("http://pageobjectpattern.wordpress.com/wp-
admin/edit.php");
            WebElement postsContainer = driver.findElement(By.id("the-
list"));
            List postsList = postsContainer.findElements(By.
tagName("tr"));
System.out.println(postsList.size());
    }
}
```

The following is the sequence of steps that the preceding test script follows to count the number of posts currently available on our blog:

1. Log in to the Admin portal.
2. Go to the **All Posts** page.
3. Count the number of posts available.

In the previous three test scripts, we log in to WordPress and perform some actions, such as creating a post, deleting a post, and counting the number of existing posts. Imagine that the ID of an element on the login page has changed, and we have to modify that in all the three, different test cases; or, if the **All Posts** page has changed, that we have to edit all the three test cases to reflect the new changes. Instead of three cases, if you have 50 test cases, changing each of them every time there is a change in the target application is very difficult. For this purpose, you need to design a test framework that keeps the changes that you need to make the test cases to a minimum. The PageObject pattern is one such design pattern that can be used to design your test framework.

What is the PageObject pattern?

Whenever we are designing an automation framework for testing web applications, we have to accept the fact that the target application and its elements are bound to change. An efficient framework is one that needs minimal refactoring to adapt to new changes in the target application. Let us try to build the preceding test scenarios into the PageObject design pattern model. Let us first start building a PageObject for the login page. This should look as shown in the following code:

```
public class AdminLoginPage {
    WebDriver driver;
    WebElement email;
    WebElement password;
    WebElement submit;
    public AdminLoginPage(WebDriver driver){
        this.driver = driver;
        driver.get("http://pageobjectpattern.wordpress.com/wp-
admin");
email = driver.findElement(By.id("user_login"));
password = driver.findElement(By.id("user_pass"));
submit = driver.findElement(By.id("wp-submit"));
    }
    public void login(){
        email.sendKeys("pageobjectpattern@gmail.com");
        password.sendKeys("webdriver123");
        submit.click();
    }
}
```

So, all the elements that are part of the process of signing in are listed in the `AdminLoginPage` class and there is a method named `login()` which manages the populating of these elements and submitting the login form. Thus, this `AdminLoginPageobject` class will represent WordPress's administration login page, constituting all the elements that are listed on the page as member variables and all the actions that can be taken on the page as methods. Now, let us see how we need to refactor the test case so far to use our newly created PageObject. Let us consider the following `TestAddNewPost` test case:

```
public class TestAddNewPostUsingPageObject {
    public static void main(String... args) {
        WebDriver driver = new FirefoxDriver();
        // Login to Admin portal
        AdminLoginPage admLoginPage = new AdminLoginPage(driver);
        admLoginPage.login();
        // Go to New Posts page
        driver.get("http://pageobjectpattern.wordpress.com/wp-admin/edit.php");
        WebElement addNewPost = driver.findElement(By.linkText("Add New"));
        addNewPost.click();
        // Add New Post
        driver.switchTo().frame("content_ifr");
        WebElement postBody = driver.findElement(By.id("tinymce"));
        postBody.sendKeys("This is description");
        driver.switchTo().defaultContent();
        WebElement title = driver.findElement(By.id("title"));
        title.click();
        title.sendKeys("My First Post");
        WebElement publish = driver.findElement(By.id("publish"));
        publish.click();
    }
}
```

In the preceding test case, the entire code for logging in to the admin page is contained in just two lines:

```
AdminLoginPage admLoginPage = new AdminLoginPage(driver);
admLoginPage.login();
```

Navigating to the admin login page, identifying the elements, providing values for the elements, and submitting the form—everything is taken care of by the PageObject. Thus, from now on, the test case need not be refactored for any changes to the admin page in the future. You just have to change the PageObject and all the test cases using this PageObject will start using the new changes without even knowing they occured.

Now that you have seen what a PageObject looks like, the Selenium library provides even more convenient ways to implement your PageObjects. Let us see them here.

Using the @FindBy annotation

An element in the PageObject is marked with the @FindBy annotation. It is used to direct the WebDriver to locate that element on a page. It takes the locating mechanism (that is, By Id or Name or Class Name) and the value of the element for that locating mechanism as input.

There are two ways of using the @FindBy annotation:

Usage 1 is shown as follows:

```
@FindBy(id="user_login")
WebElement userId;
```

Usage 2 is shown as follows:

```
@FindBy(how=How.ID, using="user_login")
WebElement userId;
```

The preceding two usages direct the WebDriver to locate the element using the locating mechanism ID with the value user_login and assigns that element to the WebElement userId. In usage 2, we have used the enumeration How. This enumeration supports all the different locating mechanisms that our By class supports. The enumeration constants supported in the How enumeration are as follows:

- **CLASS_NAME**
- **CSS**
- **ID**
- **ID_OR_NAME**
- **LINK_TEXT**
- **NAME**
- **PARTIAL_LINK_TEXT**
- **TAG_NAME**
- **XPATH**

Using the How enumeration, we will see how our AdminLoginPage class changes:

```
public class AdminLoginPage {
    WebDriver driver;
    @FindBy(how=How.ID, id="user_login")
    WebElement email;
    @FindBy(how=How.ID, id="user_pass")
    WebElement password;
    @FindBy(how=How.ID, id="wp-submit")
    WebElement submit;
    public AdminLoginPage(WebDriver driver){
        this.driver = driver;
        driver.get("http://pageobjectpattern.wordpress.com/wp-
admin");
    }
    public void login(){
        email.sendKeys("pageobjectpattern@gmail.com");
        password.sendKeys("webdriver123");
        submit.click();
    }
}
```

When the test case instantiates the preceding class in the constructor, we navigate to the WordPress login page using the following code specifed in the constructor:

```
driver.get("http://pageobjectpattern.wordpress.com/wp-admin");
```

Once the driver state is set to this page, all the FindBy declared elements, that is, email, password, and submit, are initialized by the WebDriver using the locating mechanisms specified in the FindBy annotation.

Understanding PageFactory

Another important class that the WebDriver library provides to support the PageObject pattern is the PageFactory class. Once the PageObject class declares elements using the FindBy annotation, you can instantiate that PageObject class and its elements using the PageFactory class. This class supports a static method named initElements. The API syntax for this method is as follows:

```
initElements(WebDriver driver, java.lang.Class PageObjectClass)
```

Now, let us see how this can be used in our test case to create AdminLoginPage:

```
public class TestAddNewPostUsingPageObjects {
    public static void main(String... args){
```

```
        WebDriver driver = new FirefoxDriver();
        AdminLoginPage loginPage
    = PageFactory.initElements(driver, AdminLoginPage.class);
    loginPage.login();
        }
    }
```

The `PageFactory` class instantiates the `AdminLoginPage` class and gives it the `driver` instance. The `AdminLoginPage` PageObject navigates the `driver` instance to a URL (`http://pageobjectpattern.wordpress.com/wp-admin`, in this case) and then populates all its elements annotated with the `FindBy` annotation.

Good practices for the PageObjects design

So, now that you have seen what a simple implementation of PageObject looks like, it's time to consider some good practices in designing PageObjects for your test framework.

Consider a web page as a services provider

At a high level, when you look at a page in a web application, it is nothing but an aggregation of various User Services in one place. For example, if you take a look at the **All Posts** page in our WordPress Admin console, there are many sections in it, as shown in the following screenshot:

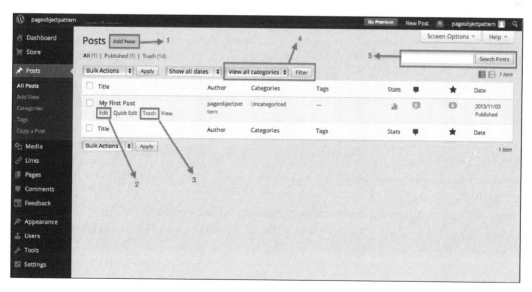

In the preceding **All Posts** page, a user can perform the following five different activities:

- Add a New post.
- Edit a selected post.
- Delete a selected post.
- Filter the posts seen by category.
- Search for some desired text in all the posts.

The preceding activities are nothing but the services that the **All Posts** page provides to its users. So, your PageObject should also provide these services to the test case, which is the user of this PageObject. The code for the **All Posts** PageObject should look as follows:

```java
public class AllPostsPage {
    WebDriver driver;
    @FindBy(how=How.ID, using="the-list")
    WebElement postsContainer;
    @FindBy(how=How.ID, using="post-search-input")
    WebElement searchPosts;
    @FindBy(how=How.ID, using="cat")
    WebElement viewByCategories;
    public AllPostsPage(WebDriver driver){
        this.driver = driver;
            driver.get("http://pageobjectpattern.wordpress.com/wp-
admin/edit.php");
    }
    public void createANewPost(String title, String description) {
    }
    public void editAPost(String title){
    }
    public void deleteAPost(String postTitle) {
    }
    public void filterPostsByCategory(String category){
    }
    public void searchInPosts(String searchText){
    }
}
```

Now, we have mapped the identified services on the page to the methods in our PageObject. When a test case wants to execute a service, it will take assistance from the PageObject to accomplish that.

Always look for implied services

There are services that a page provides which can be identified very clearly on it. But, there are some such services that are not visible on the page, but are implied. For example, in the **All Posts** page, we have identified five services just by looking at the page. But let us say your test case wants to know the count of existing posts; this information is available on the **All Posts** page, and we have to make sure that your PageObject provides that as an implied service. Now, you extend your PageObject for the **All Posts** page with this implied service, which looks as follows:

```
public class AllPostsPage {
    WebDriver driver;
    @FindBy(how=How.ID, using="the-list")
    WebElement postsContainer;
    @FindBy(how=How.ID, using="post-search-input")
    WebElement searchPosts;
    @FindBy(how=How.ID, using="cat")
    WebElement viewByCategories;
    public AllPostsPage(WebDriver driver){
        this.driver = driver;
            driver.get("http://pageobjectpattern.wordpress.com/wp-
admin/edit.php");
    }
    public void createANewPost(String title, String description) {
    }
    public void editAPost(String title){
    }
    public void deleteAPost(String postTitle) {
    }
    public void filterPostsByCategory(String category){
    }
    public void searchInPosts(String searchText){
    }
    public int getAllPostsCount(){
    }
}
```

Now your test cases can use the same PageObject to avail the implied services relevant to the **All Posts** page.

Using PageObjects within a PageObject

There will be many situations where you need to use PageObjects within a PageObject. Let us analyze that using a scenario on the **All Posts** page. When you click on **Add New** to add a new post, the browser actually navigates to a different page. So, you have to create two PageObjects, one for the **All Posts** page and another for the **Add New** page. Designing your PageObjects to simulate the exact behavior of our target application will keep things very clear and independent of each other. You may be able to navigate to the **Add New** page in several different ways. Creating a PageObject of its own for the **Add New** page and using it wherever needed will make your test framework adhere to good object-oriented fundamentals, and make the maintenance of your test framework easy. Let us see what using PageObjects within a PageObject will look like.

The AddNewPost PageObject

The AddNewPost PageObject adds new posts as shown in the following code:

```
public class AddNewPost {
    WebDriver driver;
    @FindBy(how=How.ID, using="content_ifr")
    WebElement newPostContentFrame;
    @FindBy(how=How.ID, using="tinymce")
    WebElement newPostContentBody;
    @FindBy(how=How.ID, using="title")
    WebElement newPostTitle;
    @FindBy(how=How.ID, using="publish")
    WebElement newPostPublish;
    public AddNewPost(WebDriver driver){
        this.driver = driver;
        System.out.println(driver.getCurrentUrl());
    }
    public void addNewPost(String title, String descContent){
        driver.switchTo().frame(newPostContentFrame);
        newPostContentBody.sendKeys(descContent);
        driver.switchTo().defaultContent();
        newPostTitle.click();
        newPostTitle.sendKeys(title);
        newPostPublish.click();
    }
}
```

The AllPostsPage PageObject

The `AllPostsPage` PageObject deals with the **All posts** page, as shown in the following code:

```java
public class AllPostsPage {
    WebDriver driver;
    @FindBy(how=How.ID, using="the-list")
    WebElement postsContainer;
    @FindBy(how=How.ID, using="post-search-input")
    WebElement searchPosts;
    @FindBy(how=How.ID, using="cat")
    WebElement viewByCategories;
    @FindBy(how=How.LINK_TEXT, using="Add New")
    WebElement addNewPost;
    public AllPostsPage(WebDriver driver){
        this.driver = driver;
        driver.get("http://pageobjectpattern.wordpress.com/wp-admin/edit.php");
    }
    public void createANewPost(String title, String description) {
        addNewPost.click();
        AddNewPost newPost = PageFactory.initElements(driver,
AddNewPost.class);
        newPost.addNewPost(title, description);
    }
    public void editAPost(String title){
    }
    public void deleteAPost(String postTitle) {
    }
    public void filterPostsByCategory(String category){
    }
    public void searchInPosts(String searchText){
    }
    public int getAllPostsCount(){
    }
}
```

Now, if you observe in the `AllPostsPage` PageObject, we have instantiated the `AddNewPage` PageObject in the `createNewPost()` method. Thus, we are using one PageObject with another and keeping the behavior as close as possible to the target application.

Consider methods in PageObjects as services and not as User Actions

There might sometimes be confusion surrounding what methods make a PageObject. We have seen earlier that each PageObject should contain **User Services** as their methods. But quite often, we see some implementations of PageObjects in several test frameworks that constitute User Actions as their methods. So what is the difference between a User Service and User Action? As we have already seen, some of the examples of User Services on the WordPress Admin console are as follows:

- Create a new post
- Delete a post
- Edit a post
- Search in posts
- Filter posts
- Count all existing posts

All the preceding services talk about the various functionalities of the target application. Now, let us see some of examples of User Actions.

The following are some examples of User Actions:

- Mouse click
- Typing text in a textbox
- Navigating to a page
- Clicking on a checkbox
- Select an option from a dropdown

The previous list showed some examples of User Actions on a page. They are common across many applications. Your PageObject is not meant to provide your test case with User Actions, but with User Services instead. So each method in your PageObject should map to a service that the target page provides to the user. In order to accomplish a User Service, PageObject methods should contain many User Actions.

 Several User Actions come together to accomplish a User Service.

An example of what your PageObject will look like if it provisions its methods with User Actions instead of User Services is as follows; let us see what the `AddNewPage` PageObject will look like:

```
public class AddNewPost {
    WebDriver driver;
    @FindBy(how=How.ID, using="content_ifr")
    WebElement newPostContentFrame;
    @FindBy(how=How.ID, using="tinymce")
    WebElement newPostContentBody;
    @FindBy(how=How.ID, using="title")
    WebElement newPostTitle;
    @FindBy(how=How.ID, using="publish")
    WebElement newPostPublish;
    public AddNewPost(WebDriver driver){
        this.driver = driver;
        System.out.println(driver.getCurrentUrl());
    }
    public void typeTextinTitle(String title){
        newPostTitle.sendKeys(title);
    }
    public void clickPublishButton(){
        newPostPublish.click();
    }
    public void typeTextinContent(String descContent){
        driver.switchTo().frame(newPostContentFrame);
        newPostContentBody.sendKeys(descContent);
    }
}
```

So, in the code of the `AddNewPage` PageObject, we have three different methods to accomplish three different User Actions. So the caller object, instead of just invoking the `addNewPage(String title, String description)` method, should now invoke the following:

```
typeTextinTitle(String title)
typeTextinContent(String description)
clickPublishButton()
```

The preceding User Actions are three different User Actions to accomplish adding a new post User Service. The caller of these methods should also keep in mind the order in which these User Actions need to be called; that is, the `clickPublishButton()` method should always come last. This introduces unnecessary complexity to your test cases and other PageObjects that try to add new posts in the system. Thus, User Services will hide most of the implementation details from the users of the PageObjects and reduce the cost of maintenance of your test cases.

Identifying some WebElements on the fly

In all the PageObjects, we have initialized the elements that we are going to use during object instantiation, using the @FindBy annotation. It is always good to identify all the elements of a page that are required to accomplish a User Service and assign them to the member variables in your PageObject. However, it is not always possible to do that. For example, if you want to edit a particular post in the **All Posts** page, it is not mandatory, during PageObject initialization, to map each post on the page to a member variable in your PageObject. When you have large number of posts, your PageObject initialization will be unnecessarily spending time mapping the posts to your member variables, even though we don't use them. Besides, we don't even know how many member variables we need to map all the posts in the **All Posts** page. The HTML for the **All Posts** page looks as follows:

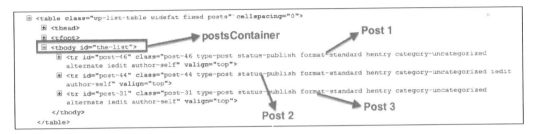

There is a root element identified by the-list, which contains all the posts in the WordPress blog. Within this element, we can see that there's Post1, Post2, and Post3. So having your PageObject initialized for all the three posts is not an optimal solution. You can initialize your PageObject with a member variable mapped to the root element and the target post will be retrieved from it whenever required.

Let us take a look at the the AllPostsPage PageObject that implements its EditPost() method in the following way:

```
public class AllPostsPage {
    WebDriver driver;
    @FindBy(how=How.ID, using="the-list")
    WebElement postsContainer;
    public void editAPost(String presentTitle,
String newTitle, String description){
        List<WebElement> allPosts
            = postsContainer.findElements(By.className("row-
title"));
        for(WebElement ele : allPosts){
            if(ele.getText().equals(presentTitle)){
```

```
            Actions builder = new Actions(driver);
            builder.moveToElement(ele);
            builder.click(driver.findElement(
                    By.cssSelector(".edit>a")));
            // Generate the composite action.
            Action compositeAction = builder.build();
            // Perform the composite action.
            compositeAction.perform();
            break;
        }
    }
        EditPost editPost
  = PageFactory.initElements(driver, EditPost.class);
        editPost.editPost(newTitle, description);
    }
}
```

Observe in the previous code that only the root element identified by the-list; the element that contains all the posts in the **All Posts** page is mapped to a member variable, named pageContainer in the AllPostsPage PageObject. The target post is extracted only when it is needed in the editAPost() method. This way, your PageObject initialization doesn't take much time and has all the necessary elements mapped.

Keeping the page-specific details off the test script

The ultimate aim of the PageObject pattern design is to maintain the page-specific details, such as the IDs of the elements on the page, the way we reach a particular page in the application, and so on, away from the test script. Building your test framework using the PageObject pattern should allow you to keep your test scripts very generic and needing no modification each time the page implementation details change. Finally whenever there is a change done to a web page, say a login page, the number of changes that need to be done for 50 test scripts that use this page should be ideally zero. Just changing the PageObject should handle adapting all the tests to the new changes.

Understanding loadable components

The loadable component is an extension to the PageObject pattern. The LoadableComponent class in the WebDriver library will help test case developers make sure that the page or a component of the page is loaded successfully. It tremendously reduces the efforts to debug your test cases. The PageObject should extend this LoadableComponent abstract class and, as a result, it is bound to provide implementation for the following two methods:

```
protected abstract void load()
protected abstract void isLoaded() throws java.lang.Error
```

The page or component that has to be loaded in the load() and isLoaded() methods determines whether or not the page or component is fully loaded. If it is not fully loaded, it throws an error.

Let us now modify the AdminLoginPage PageObject to extend the LoadableComponent class and see how it looks, using the following code:

```
package com.packt.webdriver.chapter9.pageObjects;
import org.junit.Assert;
import org.openqa.selenium.WebDriver;
import org.openqa.selenium.WebElement;
import org.openqa.selenium.support.CacheLookup;
import org.openqa.selenium.support.FindBy;
import org.openqa.selenium.support.How;
import org.openqa.selenium.support.PageFactory;
import org.openqa.selenium.support.ui.LoadableComponent;
public class AdminLoginPageUsingLoadableComponent extends LoadableComp
onent<AdminLoginPageUsingLoadableComponent>{
    WebDriver driver;
    @FindBy(how=How.ID, using="user_login")
    WebElement email;
    @FindBy(how=How.ID, using="user_pass")
    WebElement password;
    @FindBy(how=How.ID, using="wp-submit")
    WebElement submit;
    public AdminLoginPageUsingLoadableComponent(WebDriver driver){
        this.driver = driver;
        PageFactory.initElements(driver, this);
    }
    public AllPostsPage login(){
        email.sendKeys("pageobjectpattern@gmail.com");
        password.sendKeys("webdriver123");
        submit.click();
        return PageFactory.initElements(driver,
```

```
                    AllPostsPage.class);
    }
    @Override
    protected void load() {
        driver.get("http://pageobjectpattern.wordpress.com/wp-
admin");
    }
    @Override
    protected void isLoaded() throws Error {
        Assert.assertTrue(driver.getCurrentUrl().contains("wp-
admin"));
    }
}
```

The URL that has to be loaded is specified in the `load()` method and the `isLoaded()` method validates whether or not the correct page is loaded. Now, the changes that are to be done in your test case are as follows:

```
AdminLoginPageUsingLoadableComponent loginPage
        = new AdminLoginPageUsingLoadableComponent(driver).get();
```

The `get()` method, again, from the `LoadableComponent` class will make sure the component is loaded by invoking the `isLoaded()` method.

Working on an end-to-end example of WordPress

Now that we have understood what PageObjects are, it is time to take a look at an end-to-end example that interacts and tests the WordPress Admin console. First, we will see all the PageObjects and then the test cases that use them.

Looking at all the PageObjects

Let us first see all the PageObjects that are involved in testing the WordPress Admin console.

The AdminLoginPage PageObject

The `AdminLoginPage` PageObject deals with the login page. This object has to be refactored if any changes have been made to the page in the target application, using the following code:

```
package com.packt.webdriver.chapter9.pageObjects;
import org.openqa.selenium.WebDriver;
```

```
import org.openqa.selenium.WebElement;
import org.openqa.selenium.support.CacheLookup;
import org.openqa.selenium.support.FindBy;
import org.openqa.selenium.support.How;
import org.openqa.selenium.support.PageFactory;
public class AdminLoginPage {
    WebDriver driver;
    @FindBy(how=How.ID, using="user_login")
    WebElement email;
    @FindBy(how=How.ID, using="user_pass")
    WebElement password;
    @FindBy(how=How.ID, using="wp-submit")
    WebElement submit;
    public AdminLoginPage(WebDriver driver){
        this.driver = driver;
        driver.get("http://pageobjectpattern.wordpress.com/wp-
admin");
    }
    public AllPostsPage login(){
        email.sendKeys("pageobjectpattern@gmail.com");
        password.sendKeys("webdriver123");
        submit.click();
        return PageFactory.initElements(driver,
AllPostsPage.class);
    }
}
```

The constructor of the `AdminLoginPage` PageObject accepts the WebDriver instance. This will let the test framework use the same driver instance throughout the execution across test scripts as well as PageObjects; thus, the state of the browser and web application is preserved. You will see similar constructors for all the PageObjects. Apart from the constructor, the `AdminLoginPage` PageObject provides the `login()` service. This service lets the test scripts log in to the WordPress blog and, in return, gets the `AllPostsPage` PageObject. Before returning the instance of the `AllPostsPage` PageObject, the `PageFactory` PageObject will initialize all the WebElements of the `AllPostsPage` PageObject. Thus, all of the implementation details of the `login` service are hidden from the test script, and it can work with the `AllPostsPage` PageObject.

The AllPostsPage PageObject

The `AllPostsPage` PageObject deals with the **All Posts** page, using the following code:

```
package com.packt.webdriver.chapter9.pageObjects;
import java.util.List;
```

```java
import org.openqa.selenium.By;
import org.openqa.selenium.WebDriver;
import org.openqa.selenium.WebElement;
import org.openqa.selenium.interactions.Action;
import org.openqa.selenium.interactions.Actions;
import org.openqa.selenium.support.FindBy;
import org.openqa.selenium.support.How;
import org.openqa.selenium.support.PageFactory;
public class AllPostsPage {
    WebDriver driver;
    @FindBy(how=How.ID, using="the-list")
    WebElement postsContainer;
    @FindBy(how=How.ID, using="post-search-input")
    WebElement searchPosts;
    @FindBy(how=How.ID, using="cat")
    WebElement viewByCategories;
    @FindBy(how=How.LINK_TEXT, using="Add New")
    WebElement addNewPost;
    public AllPostsPage(WebDriver driver){
        this.driver = driver;
        driver.get("http://pageobjectpattern.wordpress.com/wp-
admin/edit.php");
    }
    public void createANewPost(String title, String description){
        addNewPost.click();
        AddNewPostPage newPost = PageFactory.initElements(driver,
AddNewPostPage.class);
        newPost.addNewPost(title, description);
    }
    public void editAPost(String presentTitle, String newTitle,
String description){
        goToParticularPostPage(presentTitle);
        EditPostPage editPost = PageFactory.initElements(driver,
EditPostPage.class);
        editPost.editPost(newTitle, description);
    }
    public void deleteAPost(String title) {
        goToParticularPostPage(title);
        DeletePostPage deletePost =
PageFactory.initElements(driver, DeletePostPage.class);
        deletePost.delete();
    }
    public void filterPostsByCategory(String category){
    }
    public void searchInPosts(String searchText){
```

```
        }
    public int getAllPostsCount(){
        List<WebElement> postsList = postsContainer.findElements(By.
tagName("tr"));
        return postsList.size();
    }
    private void goToParticularPostPage(String title){
List<WebElement> allPosts
            = postsContainer.findElements(By.className("row-
title"));
        for(WebElement ele : allPosts){
            if(ele.getText().equals(title)){
                Actions builder = new Actions(driver);
                builder.moveToElement(ele);
                builder.click(driver.findElement(
                        By.cssSelector(".edit>a")));
                // Generate the composite action.
                Action compositeAction = builder.build();
                // Perform the composite action.
                compositeAction.perform();
                break;
            }
        }
    }
}
```

The `AllPostsPage` PageObject provides six services. They are as follows:

- Create a Post
- Edit a Post
- Delete a Post
- Filter posts by Category
- Search for text in posts
- Count the number of posts available.

Once the test scripts obtains an instance of this PageObject via the login service of the `AdminLoginPage` PageObject, it can use any of the six services of this PageObject and test it. If any of the implementation details change, such as the navigation to a particular post or the ID of a WebElement on this page, the test script doesn't really have to worry about it. Modifying this PageObject will apply the changes to the WordPress blog.

The AddNewPostPage PageObject

The AddNewPostPage PageObject deals with adding a new post to the blog, using the following code:

```
package com.packt.webdriver.chapter9.pageObjects;
import org.openqa.selenium.WebDriver;
import org.openqa.selenium.WebElement;
import org.openqa.selenium.support.FindBy;
import org.openqa.selenium.support.How;
public class AddNewPostPage {
    WebDriver driver;
    @FindBy(how=How.ID, using="content_ifr")
    WebElement newPostContentFrame;
    @FindBy(how=How.ID, using="tinymce")
    WebElement newPostContentBody;
    @FindBy(how=How.ID, using="title")
    WebElement newPostTitle;
    @FindBy(how=How.ID, using="publish")
    WebElement newPostPublish;
    public AddNewPostPage(WebDriver driver){
        this.driver = driver;
        System.out.println(driver.getCurrentUrl());
    }
    public void addNewPost(String title, String descContent){
        driver.switchTo().frame(newPostContentFrame);
        newPostContentBody.sendKeys(descContent);
        driver.switchTo().defaultContent();
        newPostTitle.click();
        newPostTitle.sendKeys(title);
        newPostPublish.click();
    }
}
```

The AddNewPostPage PageObject is instantiated in the createANewPost service of the AllPostsPage PageObject. This PageObject provides a service named addNewPost that takes inputs for title and description for the post and publishes a new post in the blog with them.

The EditPostPage PageObject

The EditPostPage PageObject deals with editing an existing post, using the following code:

```
package com.packt.webdriver.chapter9.pageObjects;
import org.openqa.selenium.WebDriver;
import org.openqa.selenium.WebElement;
```

```
import org.openqa.selenium.support.FindBy;
import org.openqa.selenium.support.How;
public class EditPostPage {
WebDriver driver;
    @FindBy(how=How.ID, using="content_ifr")
    WebElement newPostContentFrame;
    @FindBy(how=How.ID, using="tinymce")
    WebElement newPostContentBody;
    @FindBy(how=How.ID, using="title")
    WebElement newPostTitle;
    @FindBy(how=How.ID, using="publish")
    WebElement newPostPublish;
    public EditPostPage(WebDriver driver){
        this.driver = driver;
        System.out.println(driver.getCurrentUrl());
    }
    public void editPost(String title, String descContent){
        driver.switchTo().frame(newPostContentFrame);
        newPostContentBody.clear();
        newPostContentBody.sendKeys(descContent);
        driver.switchTo().defaultContent();
        newPostTitle.click();
        newPostTitle.clear();
        newPostTitle.sendKeys(title);
        newPostPublish.click();
    }
}
```

The EditPostPage PageObject is similar to the AddNewPostPage PageObject and is instantiated at the editAPost service of the AllPostsPage PageObject. This provides a service named editPost to edit an existing post. The new title and description are passed as input parameters to this service.

The DeletePostPage PageObject

The DeletePostPage PageObject deals with deleting an existing post, using the following code:

```
package com.packt.webdriver.chapter9.pageObjects;
import org.openqa.selenium.WebDriver;
import org.openqa.selenium.WebElement;
import org.openqa.selenium.support.FindBy;
import org.openqa.selenium.support.How;
public class DeletePostPage {
WebDriver driver;
```

```
@FindBy(how=How.LINK_TEXT, using="Move to Trash")
WebElement moveToTrash;
public DeletePostPage(WebDriver driver){
    this.driver = driver;
    System.out.println(driver.getCurrentUrl());
}
public void delete(){
    moveToTrash.click();
}
}
```

The DeletePostPage PageObject is similar to AddNewPostPage and EditPostPage PageObjects and is instantiated at the deleteAPost service of the AllPostsPage PageObject. This provides a service named delete to delete an existing post.

As you can see, the AddNewPostPage, EditPostPage, and DeletePostPage PageObjects take you to the same page. So, it makes sense to merge all these three PageObjects into one that provides services for adding, editing, and deleting posts.

Looking at the test cases

Now it is time to see the test cases that use the PageObjects discussed earlier to interact with the WordPress Admin console.

Adding a new post

This test case deals with adding a new post to the blog, using the following code:

```
package com.packt.webdriver.chapter9;
import org.openqa.selenium.WebDriver;
import org.openqa.selenium.chrome.ChromeDriver;
import org.openqa.selenium.support.PageFactory;
import com.packt.webdriver.chapter9.pageObjects.AdminLoginPage;
import com.packt.webdriver.chapter9.pageObjects.AllPostsPage;
public class TestAddNewPostUsingPageObjects {
    public static void main(String... args){
        WebDriver driver = new FirefoxDriver();
        AdminLoginPage loginPage =
PageFactory.initElements(driver, AdminLoginPage.class);
        AllPostsPage allPostsPage = loginPage.login();
        allPostsPage.createANewPost("Creating New Post using
PageObjects",
                "Its good to use PageObjects");
    }
}
```

The following is the sequence of steps executed in the preceding test script to test how to add a new post to the WordPress blog:

1. First, the test script creates a `FirefoxDriver` instance, because it intends to test the scenario of adding a new post to the blog on the Firefox browser.

2. Then, it creates an instance of the `AdminLoginPage` PageObject that uses the same driver instance created in the previous step.

3. Once it gets the instance of the `AdminLoginPage` PageObject, it uses the `login` service to log in to the WordPress admin console. The `login` service, in return, gives out an instance of the `AllPostsPage` PageObject instance to the test script.

4. The test script uses the instance of the `AllPostsPage` PageObject obtained in the previous step to use one of the many services provided by the **All Posts** page. In this case, it uses the `createANewPost` service.

Editing a post

This test case deals with the testing and editing of a post in the blog using the following code:

```
package com.packt.webdriver.chapter9;
import org.openqa.selenium.WebDriver;
import org.openqa.selenium.chrome.ChromeDriver;
import org.openqa.selenium.support.PageFactory;
import com.packt.webdriver.chapter9.pageObjects.AdminLoginPage;
import com.packt.webdriver.chapter9.pageObjects.AllPostsPage;
public class TestEditPostUsingPageObjects {
    public static void main(String... args){
        System.setProperty("webdriver.chrome.driver",
"C:\\chromedriver_win32_2.2\\chromedriver.exe");
        WebDriver driver = new ChromeDriver();
        AdminLoginPage loginPage =
PageFactory.initElements(driver,
                AdminLoginPage.class);
        AllPostsPage allPostsPage = loginPage.login();
        allPostsPage.editAPost("Creating New Post using
PageObjects",
                "Editing Post using PageObjects","Test framework
low maintenance");
    }
}
```

The following is the sequence of steps executed in this test script to test the editing of a post in the WordPress blog:

1. First, the test script creates a ChromeDriver instance, because it intends to test this scenario of editing a post in the blog on the Chrome browser.

2. Then, it creates an instance of the AdminLoginPage PageObject that uses the driver instance created in the previous step.

3. Once it gets the instance of the AdminLoginPage PageObject, it uses the login service to log in to the WordPress Admin console. The login service, in return, gives out an instance of the AllPostsPage PageObject instance to the test script.

4. The test script uses the instance of the AllPostsPage PageObject obtained in the previous step to use one of the many services provided by the **All Posts** page. In this case, it uses the editAPost service.

Deleting a post

This test case deals with deleting a post, using the following code:

```
package com.packt.webdriver.chapter9;
import org.openqa.selenium.WebDriver;
import org.openqa.selenium.chrome.ChromeDriver;
import org.openqa.selenium.support.PageFactory;
import com.packt.webdriver.chapter9.pageObjects.AdminLoginPage;
import com.packt.webdriver.chapter9.pageObjects.AllPostsPage;
public class TestDeleteAPostUsingPageObjects {
    public static void main(String... args){
        System.setProperty("webdriver.chrome.driver",
"C:\\chromedriver_win32_2.2\\chromedriver.exe");
        WebDriver driver = new ChromeDriver();
        AdminLoginPage loginPage =
PageFactory.initElements(driver,
                AdminLoginPage.class);
        AllPostsPage allPostsPage = loginPage.login();
        allPostsPage.deleteAPost("Creating New Post using
PageObjects");
    }
}
```

The following is the sequence of steps executed in the preceding test script to test the deleting of a post in the WordPress blog:

1. First, the test script creates a ChromeDriver instance, because it intends to test this scenario of editing a post in the blog on the Chrome browser.

2. Then, it creates an instance of the AdminLoginPage PageObject that uses the same driver instance created in the previous step.

3. Once it gets the instance of the AdminLoginPage PageObject, it uses the login service to log in to the WordPress Admin console. The login service, in return, gives out an instance of the AllPostsPage PageObject instance to the test script.

4. The test script uses the instance of the AllPostsPage PageObject obtained in the previous step to use one of the many services provided by the **All Posts** page. In this case, it uses the deleteAPost service.

Counting posts

This test case deals with the counting of posts currently available in the blog, using the following code:

```
package com.packt.webdriver.chapter9;
import org.openqa.selenium.WebDriver;
import org.openqa.selenium.chrome.ChromeDriver;
import org.openqa.selenium.support.PageFactory;
import com.packt.webdriver.chapter9.pageObjects.AdminLoginPage;
import com.packt.webdriver.chapter9.pageObjects.AllPostsPage;
public class TestPostsCountUsingPageObjects {
    public static void main(String... args){
        System.setProperty("webdriver.chrome.driver",
"C:\\chromedriver_win32_2.2\\chromedriver.exe");
        WebDriver driver = new ChromeDriver();
        AdminLoginPage loginPage =
PageFactory.initElements(driver,
                AdminLoginPage.class);
        AllPostsPage allPostsPage = loginPage.login();
        System.out.println(allPostsPage.getAllPostsCount());
    }
}
```

The following is the sequence of steps executed in the preceding test script to test the counting of the number of posts in the WordPress blog:

1. First, the test script creates a `ChromeDriver` instance, because it intends to test this scenario of editing a post in the blog on Chrome browser.

2. Then, it creates an instance of the `AdminLoginPage` PageObject that uses the driver instance created in the previous step.

3. Once it gets the instance of the `AdminLoginPage` PageObject, it uses the `login` service to log in to the WordPress Admin console. The `login` service, in return, gives out an instance of the `AllPostsPage` PageObject instance to the test script.

4. The test script uses the instance of the `AllPostsPage` PageObject obtained in the previous step to use one of the many services provided by the **All Posts** page. In this case, it uses the `getAllPostsCount` service.

Summary

In this chapter, we have seen what a PageObject pattern is and how we can implement a test framework using PageObjects. We have seen numerous advantages of this. The PageObject pattern and the `LoadableComponents` class provides the test framework to adapt easily to changes made to the target application, without changing any test cases. We should always remember that a better-designed test framework is always flexible to changes made to the target application.

In the next chapter, we will look at testing iOS and Android mobile applications.

10
Testing iOS and Android Apps

In all our previous chapters, we have worked on web applications that are loaded in desktop browsers. But with the increasing number of mobile users, businesses today have to serve their users on mobile devices as well. In this chapter, we will take a look at the available software tools in the market that make use of Selenium WebDriver, which help us test our applications on iOS and Android platforms.

Different forms of mobile applications

There are three different forms in which an application can reach a user on the mobile platform. They are as follows:

- **Native apps**: Native apps are purely specific to the target mobile platform. They are developed in the platform-supported languages and are very much tied to underlying SDKs. For iOS, applications are developed in Objective-C and are dependent on iOS SDK; similarly, for the Android platform, they are developed in Java and are dependent on Android SDK.

- **m.site**: m.site, also known as mobile website, on the other hand, is a mini version of your web application that loads on the browsers of your mobile devices. On iOS devices, it can be Safari or Chrome, and on Android devices, it can be the Android default browser or Chrome.

For example, on your iOS or Android device, open your browser and type in www.facebook.com. Before the page loads, you will observe that a URL redirection happens from www.facebook.com to m.facebook.com. Facebook application servers realize that the request has originated from a mobile device and start servicing its mobile site rather than the regular desktop site.

These m.sites use JavaScript and HTML5 to be developed just as your normal web applications.

- **Hybrid apps**: The Hybrid app is a combination of the native app and web app. When you develop a native app, some parts of it load HTML web pages into the app trying to make the user feel he/she is using a native application. They generally use **WebViews** in native apps to load the web pages.

Now, you as a test scripts developer, have to test all these different applications on various mobile devices.

Available software tools

In order to automate the testing of your applications on mobile devices, there are many software tools available. The following are some of the tools that are built based on Selenium WebDriver:

- **AndroidDriver**: This driver is a direct implementation of WebDriver, which is similar to FirefoxDriver, IEDriver, and so on. It acts as the client library with which your test script interacts. Its server side is the AndroidWebDriver that is installed on the device, or the emulator and executes all the test script commands that gets forwarded from AndroidDriver.

- **iPhoneDriver**: This driver works very similar to AndroidDriver, but only on iOS platforms. In order to use it, you need to set up a server on the simulator or on the device. iPhoneDriver, however, is no longer supported and is deprecated.

- **iOSDriver**: As the name says, this driver is used for automating native, hybrid, and m.site applications on iOS platforms. It uses native UI Automation libraries to automate on the iOS platform. For the test scripts, all this is transparent because it can still continue to use the WebDriver API in its favorite client language bindings. The test script communicates with the iOS Driver using the JSON wire protocol. However, if you want to execute your test scripts against the Android platform, you cannot use this driver.

- **Selendroid**: This driver is similar to iOSDriver and can execute your native, hybrid, and m.site application test scripts on the Android platform. It uses the native UI Automator library provided by Google. The test scripts communicate with the Selendroid driver over the JSON wire protocol while using its favorite client language bindings.

- **Appium:** This is another tool that can let you execute your test scripts against Android and iOS platforms without your having to change the underlying driver. Appium can also work with Firefox OS platforms. In the rest of the chapter, we will see how we can work with Appium.

Automating iOS and Android tests using Appium

Appium is an upcoming tool that can be used to automate your test scripts for both Android and iOS platforms. It can be used to automate native, m.sites, and hybrid applications. It internally uses WebDriver's JSON wire protocol.

Automating iOS application tests

For automating iOS app tests, Appium uses Apple Instruments. According to Apple, Instruments is a performance, analysis, and testing tool for dynamically tracing and profiling OS X and iOS code. It is a flexible and powerful tool that lets you track one or more processes and examine the collected data. In this way, Instruments helps you understand the behavior of both user apps and the operating system. In particular, Appium uses UI Automation Instrument. UI Automation Instrument is used to automate user interface tests of iOS apps. More information about this instrument can be found at `https://developer.apple.com/library/mac/documentation/DeveloperTools/Conceptual/InstrumentsUserGuide/UsingtheAutomationInstrument/UsingtheAutomationInstrument.html`.

Appium works as a Remote WebDriver and receives the commands from your test scripts over JSON wire protocol. These commands are passed to Apple Instruments to be executed on the native app launched on a simulator or a real device. Before the commands are passed on to the Apple Instruments, Appium translates the JSON commands into UI Automation JavaScript commands that are understood by Instruments. Apple Instruments will launch your app on the simulator or real device and start executing your test script commands on it. This process is shown in the following diagram:

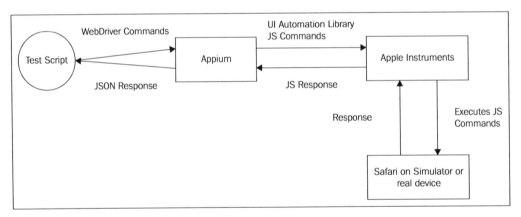

After the command is executed against your app on the simulator or device, the target app sends the response to the Instruments, which are transferred to Appium in the JavaScript response format. Appium translates the UI Automation JavaScript responses into Selenium WebDriver JSON wire protocol responses and sends them back to your test script.

The main advantages of using Appium for your iOS automation testing are as follows:

- It uses the iOS platform-supported UI Automation library and Instruments provided by Apple itself.

- Even though you are using the JavaScript library, your tests and you as a test script developer are not really tied to it. You can use your own Selenium WebDriver client-language bindings, such as Java, Ruby, Python, and so on, to develop your test scripts. Appium will take care of translating them into JavaScript for you.

- You don't have to modify your native or hybrid apps for the purpose of testing.

Automating Android application tests

Automating Android tests for your Android apps is similar to automating iOS apps tests. Except for the fact that your target platform is changing, your test scripts would not undergo any change. The following is the diagram that shows the workflow:

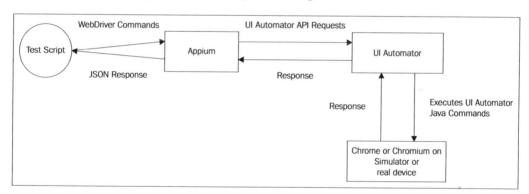

Again, Appium works as a Remote WebDriver and receives the commands from your test scripts over the JSON wire protocol. These commands are passed to Google UI Automator, which comes with Android SDK, to be executed on the native app launched on a simulator or a real device. Before the commands are passed on the UI Automator, Appium translates the JSON commands into UI Automator commands that are understood by UI Automator. This UI Automator will launch your app on the simulator or real device and start executing your test script commands on it. After the command is executed against your app on the simulator or device, the target app sends the response to the UI Automator, which is transferred to Appium in the UI Automator response format. Appium translates the UI Automator responses into Selenium WebDriver JSON wire protocol responses and sends them back to your test script.

This is the high-level architecture that helps you understand how Appium works with Android and iOS devices to execute your test commands.

Prerequisites for Appium

Before we start discussing some working examples with Appium, we need to install some prerequisite tools for iOS and Android platforms. We need to setup Xcode and Android SDK for this purpose, for which I'll be showing the examples on Mac OS.

Setting up Xcode

To set up the Xcode, we will perform the following steps:

1. You can download the latest Xcode from `https://developer.apple.com/xcode/`.

2. After downloading it, install and open it.

3. Now navigate to **Preferences | Downloads** and install **Command Line Tools** and iOS Simulators, as shown in the following screenshot:

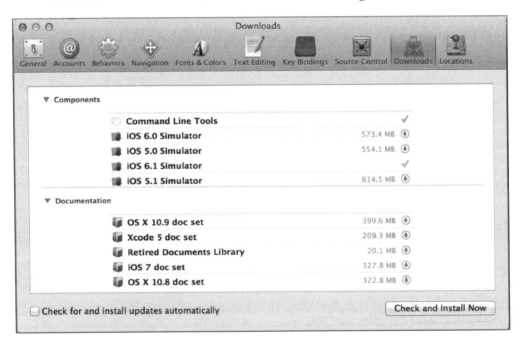

If you are using a real device, you need a provision profile installed on the device and USB debugging enabled on it.

Try to launch the iPhone simulator and verify that it works. You can launch the simulator by navigating to **Xcode | Open Developer Tool | iOS Simulator**. The simulator should look similar to what is shown in the following screenshot:

Setting up Android SDK

You need to install Android SDK from `http://developer.android.com/sdk/index.html`. Download the **Android Developer Tools (ADT)** and install.

Launch the installed ADT. Now, download any Android whose API level is 17, and install it. You can do that by navigating to **Window | Android SDK Manager**. You should see something similar to what is shown in the following screenshot:

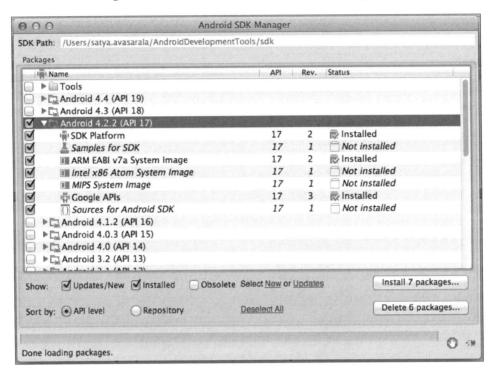

Here, we are installing Android 4.2.2, which is API level 17.

Creating Android Emulator

If you want to execute your test scripts on an Android Emulator, you have to create one. To create one, we will perform the following steps:

1. In ADT, open the Android device manager by navigating to **Windows | Android Virtual Device Manager**. It launches the AVD Manager, as shown in the following screenshot:

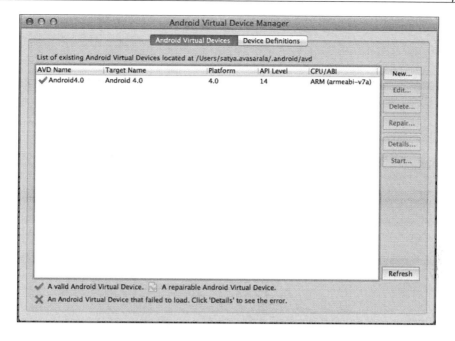

2. Now create a new virtual device or emulator by clicking on the **New** button. You should see a window that will take all the necessary information from you, as shown in the following screenshot:

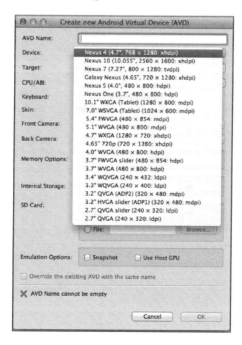

3. Launch the Emulator to see if it was created successfully. It might take several minutes for the **Android Virtual Device** to start. The following is the screenshot that shows a started Android Emulator:

Using real device for executing your tests

To use real devices for testing your application using Appium, you need to root the device. There are many online guides that can help you root your Android device.

 Rooting your Android device might devoid your warranty from your phone manufacturer. So make sure you root the devices that are meant specifically for testing and not your personal devices.

Installing Appium

You can download Appium from `http://appium.io/`. Click on the **Download Appium** button to download Appium specific to your workstation platform. Here I am using Mac, so it will download the Appium DMG file of Version 0.11.4

Copy Appium to the `Applications` folder, and try to launch it. The first time it is launched, it asks for your authorization to run the iOS simulators, as shown in the following screenshot:

After you grant the authorization, click on **Launch** to start the Appium server. By default, it starts at `http://localhost:4723`. This is the remote URL to which your test scripts should be using to direct the test commands.

Automating for iOS

Let's see what happens internally when we try to execute our `RemoteWebDriver` test script for automating the Google Search page:

```java
import java.net.MalformedURLException;
import java.net.URL;
import org.openqa.selenium.By;
import org.openqa.selenium.WebDriver;
import org.openqa.selenium.WebElement;
import org.openqa.selenium.remote.DesiredCapabilities;
import org.openqa.selenium.remote.RemoteWebDriver;
public class AppiumiOS {
    public static void main(String... args){
        DesiredCapabilities desiredCapabilities = new
DesiredCapabilities();
        desiredCapabilities.setCapability("device", "iPhone
Simulator");
        desiredCapabilities.setCapability("version", "7.0");
        desiredCapabilities.setCapability("app", "safari");
        URL url = null;
        try {
            url = new URL("http://127.0.0.1:4723/wd/hub");
        } catch (MalformedURLException e) {
            // TODO Auto-generated catch block
            e.printStackTrace();
        }
        WebDriver remoteWebDriver = new RemoteWebDriver(url,
 desiredCapabilities);
        remoteWebDriver.get("http://www.google.com");
        WebElement ele =
 remoteWebDriver.findElement(By.name("q"));
        ele.click();
        ele.sendKeys("Packt Publishing");
        WebElement searchButton =
 remoteWebDriver.findElement(By.name("btnG"));
        System.out.println(searchButton.getSize());
        searchButton.click();
        remoteWebDriver.quit();
    }
}
```

If you observe, the preceding code is very much similar to the test script for `RemoteWebDriver`. However, there are a few differences though. The following code depicts that:

```
desiredCapabilities.setCapability("device", "iPhone Simulator");
desiredCapabilities.setCapability("version", "7.0");
desiredCapabilities.setCapability("app", "safari");
```

The preceding code is the set of desired capabilites that we specify to help Appium decide on which the platform our test script should get executed.

```
desiredCapabilities.setCapability("device", "iPhone Simulator");
```

The preceding code informs Appium that we need to use the iPhone simulator. If we want to use the iPad simulator, the capability will look like the following:

```
desiredCapabilities.setCapability("device", "iPad Simulator");
```

If we want to use a real device, we just have to specify iPhone or iPad. Appium will pick the device that is connected to the Mac via USB.

The second desired capability that we have mentioned is the version of the iPhone simulator to use:

```
desiredCapabilities.setCapability("version", "7.0");
```

Here we are using the iOS 7.0 simulator. At the time of writing this book, Appium works with iOS7 simulators with Xcode 5, and iOS6.1 simulators with Xcode 4.6.

The third desired capability is shown in the following code:

```
desiredCapabilities.setCapability("app", "safari");
```

In the preceding code, we point Appium to the target application. Here, we mention the path to our native or hybrid app. In our test script, while we are loading `http://www.google.com` in a Safari browser, we are asking Appium to launch the Safari app already existing on the simulator.

And finally, our test script is trying to connect to the Appium Server on port `4723`, as shown in the following code:

```
url = new URL("http://127.0.0.1:4723/wd/hub");
```

We start creating a `RemoteWebDriver` instance with the Appium server in our test script using the following code:

```
WebDriver remoteWebDriver = new RemoteWebDriver(url,
desiredCapabilities);
```

The following log output is what the Appium tries to do:

```
info: instruments is: /Applications/Xcode.app/Contents/Developer/usr/bin/instruments

info: [INSTSERVER] Instruments socket server started at /tmp/instruments_sock
info: Spawning instruments with command: /Applications/Xcode.app/Contents/Developer/usr/bin/instruments -t /
Applications/Xcode.app/Contents/Applications/Instruments.app/Contents/PlugIns/AutomationInstrument.bundle/
Contents/Resources/Automation.tracetemplate /var/folders/cq/ccxtfs8n6pl_5q6m2qtf25qxkxjlq9/T/
1131017-54506-1u8drzz/submodules/SafariLauncher/build/Release-iphonesimulator/SafariLauncher.app -e UIASCRIPT /
Applications/Appium.app/Contents/Resources/node_modules/appium/lib/devices/ios/uiauto/bootstrap.js -e
UIARESULTSPATH /tmp/appium-instruments/
info: And extra without-delay env: {"DYLD_INSERT_LIBRARIES":"/Applications/Appium.app/Contents/Resources/
node_modules/appium/build/iwd/InstrumentsShim.dylib","LIB_PATH":"/Applications/Appium.app/Contents/Resources/
node_modules/appium/build/iwd"}
info: And launch timeout: 90000ms

debug: Appium request initiated at /wd/hub/status

info: Responding to client with success: {"status":0,"value":{"build":
{"version":"0.11.4","revision":"b04decd191002628c88e9bf475553da1cd04a036"}},"sessionId":"ec3289ee-c1fd-4d48-b217-
ea9681ba5b05"}
```

In the preceding screenshot, it tries to launch the iOS simulator, and meanwhile establishes a session with your test script. After that, the Safari app is launched on the simulator, and all our test script commands are executed on the simulator. The following is the screenshot of the simulator while it executes our test script:

Similarly, we can work on another example of m.site for Facebook. The following is the code that opens `http://www.facebook.com` on the Safari browser of the iPhone simulator where the URL is redirected to Facebook's m.site, and then the test script tries to log in:

```
public class AppiumiOSFacebook {
public static void main(String... args){
        DesiredCapabilities desiredCapabilities = new
DesiredCapabilities();
        desiredCapabilities.setCapability("device", "iPhone
Simulator");
        desiredCapabilities.setCapability("version", "7.0");
        desiredCapabilities.setCapability("app", "safari");
        URL url = null;
        try {
            url = new URL("http://127.0.0.1:4723/wd/hub");
        } catch (MalformedURLException e) {
            // TODO Auto-generated catch block
            e.printStackTrace();
        }
        WebDriver remoteWebDriver = new RemoteWebDriver(url,
desiredCapabilities);
        remoteWebDriver.get("http://www.facebook.com");
        System.out.println("The current url is:
"+remoteWebDriver.getCurrentUrl());
        WebElement email =
remoteWebDriver.findElement(By.name("email"));
        WebElement password =
remoteWebDriver.findElement(By.name("pass"));
        WebElement login =
remoteWebDriver.findElement(By.name("login"));
        email.sendKeys("test.appium@gmail.com");
        password.sendKeys("123456");
        login.click();
        remoteWebDriver.quit();
    }
}
```

The output for the next line of code is shown in the following screenshot.

```
System.out.println("The current url is:
"+remoteWebDriver.getCurrentUrl());
```

The current url is: https://m.facebook.com/?refsrc=http%3A%2F%2Fwww.apple.com%2F&_rdr

The following is the screenshot of the Facebook login page being loaded on Safari in the iPhone simulator:

Automating for Android

Until now, we have seen how to automate our test scripts that use the Appium server and iOS simulators. Now, we shall work on Android. Here, we will try to execute our test scripts on the Android real device. We need to make sure we have installed Chrome on our Android device and connect our device to our machine. Now, we navigate to our `ANDROID_HOME/sdk/platform-tools` and execute the following code:

```
./adb devices
```

Android Debug Bridge (adb), is a command-line tool that lets you communicate with the Android emulator or real device. All the Android devices that are connected to the host will be listed. Here, we've attached one device to our machine, and the output is as follows:

List of devices attached

4df1e76f39e54f43   device

The hex code is the connected device's ID, and **device** in the listing says the listed is a real device and not an emulator.

The following is the test script for automating the Google Search page on the Android device:

```
public class AppiumAndroid {
public static void main(String... args){
        DesiredCapabilities desiredCapabilities
                    = new  DesiredCapabilities();
        desiredCapabilities.setCapability("device", "Android");
        desiredCapabilities.setCapability("app", "chrome");
        URL url = null;
        try {
            url = new URL("http://127.0.0.1:4723/wd/hub");
        } catch (MalformedURLException e) {
            // TODO Auto-generated catch block
            e.printStackTrace();
        }
        WebDriver remoteWebDriver = new RemoteWebDriver(url,
desiredCapabilities);
        //WebDriver remoteWebDriver = new FirefoxDriver();
        remoteWebDriver.get("http://www.google.com");
        WebElement ele =
remoteWebDriver.findElement(By.name("q"));
        ele.click();
        ele.sendKeys("Packt Publishing");
        WebElement searchButton =
remoteWebDriver.findElement(By.name("btnG"));
        System.out.println(searchButton.getSize());
        searchButton.click();
        remoteWebDriver.quit();
    }
}
```

The following is the desired capability that will allow Appium to understand that the preceding test script needs to be executed on the Android device:

```
desiredCapabilities.setCapability("device", "Android");
```

Appium will use the first device from the list of devices that adb returns. Once the device is chosen, the following desired capability will launch Chrome browser on the device and start executing the test script commands on it:

```
desiredCapabilities.setCapability("app", "chrome");
```

Summary

In this chapter, we have discussed the different ways a business can reach out to its users on mobile platforms. We also discussed the various software tools that are created based on Selenium WebDriver. And finally, we went through one of the upcoming software tools and modified our test script to work with iOS and Android platforms.

For more examples on using Appium, please visit the website and github forums at `http://appium.io/` and `https://github.com/appium/appium/tree/master/sample-code/examples`.

Index

T

takesScreenShot capability 63
TakesScreenshot interface 155
target windows
  locating 65
temporary directory
  deleting 134
temporary filesystem
  changing 135, 136
TemporaryFilesystem class
  default temporary filesystem 132
  directory, creating in DefaultTmpFS 133
  multiple files, deleting 134
  temporary directory, deleting 134
  temporary filesystem, changing 135, 136
test cases
  creating, for WordPress blog 191
Thread.sleep() method 133
throwOnCapabilityNotPresent parameter
    187
to() method 70
try-catch block 87
type attribute 26

U

unregisterIfStillDownAfter parameter 186
UsingChromeOptions class 107

V

void accept() 68
void dismiss() 68
void sendKeys(java.lang.String keys-
    ToSend) 68

W

Web Application Under Test (WAUT) 9
WebDriverBackedSelenium
  exploring 165- 167
WebDriverBackedSelenium class 139, 166
WebDriverEventListener
  implementing 115
WebDriver event listeners
  browser back navigation, listening for 122

browser forward navigation, listening for
    123
browser navigateTo events, listening for
    123
  exception, listening for 124
  script execution, listening for 123
  WebElement clicked, listening for 122
  WebElement search event, listening for 122
  WebElement value change, listening for
    121
WebDriver instance
  creating 118
WebDriver javadoc
  URL 21
WebElement action
  clickAndHold 51
  click on 49
  contextClick 57, 58
  doubleClick 57
  release on 53
WebElement, clicking
  listening for 122
WebElements
  about 20, 21
  actions 32
  By locating mechanism, using 23
  Explicit wait time 73
  findElement() method 21, 22
  findElements() method 22
  FireBug 22, 23
  identifying 206
  Implicit wait time 72
  loading 71
  locating, WebDriver used 21
WebElement search event
  listening for 122
WebElement value change
  listening for 121
web page
  considering, as service provider 199, 200
webStorageEnabled capability 63
WebViews 222
windows
  switching among 65, 66
WordPress blog
  post, adding to 192, 215

Thank you for buying
Selenium WebDriver Practical Guide

About Packt Publishing

Packt, pronounced 'packed', published its first book "*Mastering phpMyAdmin for Effective MySQL Management*" in April 2004 and subsequently continued to specialize in publishing highly focused books on specific technologies and solutions.

Our books and publications share the experiences of your fellow IT professionals in adapting and customizing today's systems, applications, and frameworks. Our solution based books give you the knowledge and power to customize the software and technologies you're using to get the job done. Packt books are more specific and less general than the IT books you have seen in the past. Our unique business model allows us to bring you more focused information, giving you more of what you need to know, and less of what you don't.

Packt is a modern, yet unique publishing company, which focuses on producing quality, cutting-edge books for communities of developers, administrators, and newbies alike. For more information, please visit our website: www.packtpub.com.

About Packt Open Source

In 2010, Packt launched two new brands, Packt Open Source and Packt Enterprise, in order to continue its focus on specialization. This book is part of the Packt Open Source brand, home to books published on software built around Open Source licences, and offering information to anybody from advanced developers to budding web designers. The Open Source brand also runs Packt's Open Source Royalty Scheme, by which Packt gives a royalty to each Open Source project about whose software a book is sold.

Writing for Packt

We welcome all inquiries from people who are interested in authoring. Book proposals should be sent to author@packtpub.com. If your book idea is still at an early stage and you would like to discuss it first before writing a formal book proposal, contact us; one of our commissioning editors will get in touch with you.

We're not just looking for published authors; if you have strong technical skills but no writing experience, our experienced editors can help you develop a writing career, or simply get some additional reward for your expertise.

Selenium 2 Testing Tools Beginner's Guide

ISBN: 978-1-84951-830-7   Paperback: 232 pages

Learn to use Selenium testing tools from scratch

1. Automate web browsers with Selenium WebDriver to test web applications.

2. Set up Java environment for using Selenium WebDriver.

3. Learn good design patterns for testing web applications.

Selenium Testing Tools Cookbook

ISBN: 978-1-84951-574-0   Paperback: 326 pages

Over 90 recipes to build, maintain, and improve test automation with Selenium WebDriver

1. Learn to leverage the power of Selenium WebDriver with simple examples that illustrate real-world problems and their workarounds.

2. Each sample demonstrates key concepts allowing you to advance your knowledge of Selenium WebDriver in a practical and incremental way.

3. Explains testing of mobile web applications with Selenium Drivers for platforms such as iOS and Android.

Please check **www.PacktPub.com** for information on our titles

Instant Selenium Testing Tools Starter

ISBN: 978-1-78216-514-9   Paperback: 52 pages

A short, fast, and focused guide to Selenium Testing tools that delivers immediate results

1. Learn something new in an Instant! A short, fast, focused guide delivering immediate results.

2. Learn to create web tests using Selenium Tools.

3. Learn to use PageObject pattern.

4. Run and analyze test results on an easy-to-use platform.

Selenium 1.0 Testing Tools Beginner's Guide

ISBN: 978-1-84951-026-4   Paperback: 232 pages

Test your web applications with multiple browsers using the Selenium Framework to ensure the quality of web applications

1. Save your valuable time by using Selenium to record, tweak, and replay your test scripts.

2. Get rid of any bugs deteriorating the quality of your web applications.

3. Take your web applications one step closer to perfection using Selenium tests.

4. Packed with detailed working examples that illustrate the techniques and tools for debugging.

Please check **www.PacktPub.com** for information on our titles

Made in the USA
Lexington, KY
08 February 2017